Mind matters

A collection of activities
and puzzles for
language learners

Alan Maley
Françoise Grellet

Cambridge University Press
Cambridge
London   New York   New Rochelle
Melbourne   Sydney

Published by the Press Syndicate of the University of Cambridge
The Pitt Building, Trumpington Street, Cambridge CB2 1RP
32 East 57th Street, New York, NY 10022, U.S.A.
296 Beaconsfield Parade, Middle Park, Melbourne 3206, Australia

First published 1981

Printed in Great Britain by
Cox & Wyman Ltd, Reading

ISBN 0 521 23389 5

Contents

To the reader

Which of these clocks is accurate more often: a clock that has stopped or a clock that gains one minute a day?
(Solution: page 103)

How can you make these five pieces of chain into one long chain by cutting and joining only three links?

If you need help, turn to the clue on page 79.   (Solution: page 88)

What has a mouth bigger than its head?   (Solution: page 85)

These questions are typical of the puzzles and problems you will find in this book.

The first part is full of ideas for tricks and puzzles you can try out on your friends.

The second part will really make you think as you try to break codes or find answers to brainteasers and riddles. For some of the more difficult problems, you may need to consult the clues at the back of the book.

Problem-solving activities are fun and can provide valuable language practice when done in pairs or small groups. Suggestions to the teacher on how the book may be used in class are given at the back of the book.

Clues and solutions

You will see a key symbol (⚷) beside some questions. This tells you that there is a clue to help you find the answer in the **Clues** section starting on p. 78. You can check your answers with the solutions given in the section beginning on p. 85, but remember – some questions are just to set you thinking and have no 'right' answer.

Part 1

1 Tricks with numbers

1.1

Ask a friend to think of a number. Then ask him to:
–multiply it by 5
–add 6
–multiply the result by 4
–add 9
–multiply the result by 5

Ask him what the result is and you will immediately be able to tell him what the number he had chosen was.

How to do it: Subtract 165 from the result and take off the two zeros at the end of the number you get. This will leave you with the original number.

1.2

Here is a mind-reading trick which will enable you to discover a person's age. Ask a friend to:
–multiply his age by 2
–add 5
–multiply the result by 50
–add the age of his father
–subtract the number of days in a year

When he gives you the result, you will tell him his age and that of his father.

How to do it: Add 115 to the number you get. The first two numbers will represent your friend's age, the last two his father's age.

1.3

Ask a friend to choose any three–digit number in which the first and last digits are different and do not add up to 9. Then tell him to:

e.g.

—reverse the first and last digits $\qquad$ $315 \rightarrow 513$

—subtract the smaller number from the larger one

$$513$$
$$315 \; -$$
$$\overline{198}$$

Ask your friend what the first digit of this number is.
You can now tell him what the other two numbers are.

How to do it: The second digit will always be 9. The sum of the first and last digits will also be 9. So, if you know the first one, subtract it from 9 to find out what the last one is.

1.4

Ask a friend to choose a three–digit number and to repeat it to get a six–digit number (e.g. $215 \rightarrow 215215$). Then ask him to:
—divide the number he has obtained by 7
—divide the new number by 11
—divide the result by 13

The result should be the original number your friend had chosen. (Your friend will be surprised when you tell him beforehand that there will be no remainder.)

1.5

Show the following magic table to a friend:

7	13	10	19	8
1	7	4	13	2
13	19	16	25	14
4	10	7	16	5
6	12	9	18	7

Ask him to choose a square and to put a button on it. Then cover all the numbers in the same horizontal and vertical lines (with little strips of paper).

Ask your friend to do the same thing with a second square (put a button on it and cover the other numbers in the same row and column). Do this again twice (choosing any square where the number is not covered) until only *one* number is left. Cover it with a button too. Then lift the five buttons. The total of the five numbers will always be 53!

You can do this again and again, choosing any numbers and you will always get 53 as a result.

Can you find out why?

1.6

Ask a friend to choose any square of nine numbers on a calendar (e.g. the ones below).

S	M	T	W	T	F	S
1	2	3	4	5	6	7
8	9	10	11	12	13	14
15	16	17	18	19	20	21

He should not tell you which square he has chosen. Ask him to tell you the lowest of the numbers. You are then able to tell him the sum of all the numbers in the square.

How to do it: Add 8 to the number he gives you and then multiply this number by 9.

1.7

Ask a friend to choose a three–digit number in which the first and last digits differ by at least two. Ask him to:

e.g.

—reverse the number

$481 \rightarrow 184$

—subtract the smaller number from the larger one

$$\begin{array}{r} 481 \\ 184 \ - \\ \hline 297 \end{array}$$

Tell him to reverse the digits of the answer and add this number to the answer.

$$\begin{array}{r} 792 \ + \\ \hline 1089 \end{array}$$

Although you did not know what number he had chosen, you will surprise him by giving him the right answer, which is always 1089.

1.8

Show the following tables to a friend and ask him to point out the one(s) in which his age appears.

2	38	74
3	39	75
6	42	78
7	43	79
10	46	82
11	47	83
14	50	86
15	51	87
18	54	90
19	55	91
22	58	94
23	59	95
26	62	98
27	63	99
30	66	102
31	67	103
34	70	106
35	71	107

1

1	37	73
3	39	75
5	41	77
7	43	79
9	45	81
11	47	83
13	49	85
15	51	87
17	53	89
19	55	91
21	57	93
23	59	95
25	61	97
27	63	99
29	65	101
31	67	103
33	69	105
35	71	107

2

64	82	100
65	83	101
66	84	102
67	85	103
68	86	104
69	87	105
70	88	106
71	89	107
72	90	
73	91	
74	92	
75	93	
76	94	
77	95	
78	96	
79	97	
80	98	
81	99	

3

4	38	76
5	39	77
6	44	78
7	45	79
12	46	84
13	47	85
14	52	86
15	53	87
20	54	92
21	55	93
22	60	94
23	61	95
28	62	100
29	63	101
30	68	102
31	69	103
36	70	
37	71	

4

8	42	76
9	43	77
10	44	78
11	45	79
12	46	88
13	47	89
14	56	90
15	57	91
24	58	92
25	59	93
26	60	94
27	61	95
28	62	104
29	63	105
30	72	106
31	73	107
40	74	
41	75	

5

32	49	98
33	50	99
34	51	100
35	52	101
36	53	102
37	54	103
38	55	104
39	56	105
40	57	106
41	58	107
42	59	
43	60	
44	61	
45	62	
46	63	
47	96	
48	97	

6

16	49	82
17	50	83
18	51	84
19	52	85
20	53	86
21	54	87
22	55	88
23	56	89
24	58	90
25	58	91
26	59	92
27	60	93
28	61	94
29	62	95
30	63	
31	80	
48	81	

7

You will then be able to tell him immediately how old he is.

How to do it: All you have to do is add up the numbers at the top of the left column of each of the tables he pointed to. They will give you the age of the person (e.g. somebody who is 34 will point to tables 1 and 6. By adding 2 and 32, you will find his age).

1.9

Ask a friend to choose two numbers and to write them one below the other.

    e.g.   5
                 3

Keep your back turned so that you cannot see what the numbers are and tell him to add them and write the sum underneath.

    e.g.   5
                 3
                 8

He must then go on adding the last two numbers until he gets to numbers in a vertical column.

    e.g.   5
                  3
                  8
              11
              19
              30
              49
              79
            128
            207

Then ask him to show you the paper and you will at once tell him what the sum is.

How to do it: Just multiply the fourth number from the bottom by 11. It can be done quickly and you will obtain the total (e.g. $49 \times 11 = 539$).

When you do this trick, you will be able to predict a final total – the sum of several numbers, some of which were given at random by your friends!

First, you have to think of the sum you want to end with.

   e.g.   21335

Write it down on a piece of paper and fold it.

Take out the first digit and add it to the remaining number (e.g. 1335 + 2 = 1337). Write this number down and ask a friend to write another four-digit number underneath.

   e.g.   1337
           6164

Then write another four-digit number underneath. Although it must look as though you are doing it at random, write under each digit its difference from 9.

   e.g.   1337
           6164
           3835

Ask another friend to select a number and write the digits adding up to 9 underneath.

   e.g.   1337
           6164
           3835
           2796
           7203

Ask a friend to add up the numbers and show him that you had predicted the sum which is the number written on the paper.

(In this case the first digit of your original number was 2, so you twice asked friends to add a number. If it had been 3, you would have asked them three times, if 4, four times, etc.)

1.11

An easy way to surprise your friends will be for you to memorise the following calculations:

$$1 \times 9 + 2 = 11$$
$$12 \times 9 + 3 = 111$$
$$123 \times 9 + 4 = 1111$$
$$1234 \times 9 + 5 = 11111$$
$$12345 \times 9 + 6 = 111111$$
$$123456 \times 9 + 7 = 1111111$$
$$1234567 \times 9 + 8 = 11111111$$
$$12345678 \times 9 + 9 = 111111111$$

$$9 \times 9 + 7 = 88$$
$$98 \times 9 + 6 = 888$$
$$987 \times 9 + 5 = 8888$$
$$9876 \times 9 + 4 = 88888$$
$$98765 \times 9 + 3 = 888888$$
$$987654 \times 9 + 2 = 8888888$$
$$9876543 \times 9 + 1 = 88888888$$
$$98765432 \times 9 + 0 = 888888888$$

1.12

Here's a trick that will make your friends think you can guess any number they think of.
- Choose a number between 0 and 50 and write it down on a piece of paper. Fold the paper and give it to a friend who mustn't look at it.
- Ask your friend to choose a number between 50 and 100. He mustn't let you know what it is.
- Subtract the number you had chosen (and written on the piece of paper) from 99.
- Ask your friend to add the result you get to the number he chose.
- He must then take off the first digit on the left and add it to the number.
- Then, ask him to subtract this number from the one he had originally chosen.

The resulting number will be the one *you* had written on the paper at the very beginning!

2 Tricks with objects

2.1 How many matches?

For this, you will need a book of matches containing exactly 20 matches.

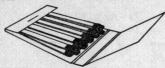

Give them to a friend and ask him to tear out a few matches (fewer than 10) while your back is turned. He should put them in his pocket.

Now ask him to count the number remaining without telling you and to tear out enough matches to form that number on the table (e.g. if there are 11 left he needs to tear out two matches – | + | ; if there are 15 left he needs to tear out six – | + | | | | | , etc.) When he has torn them out, he should put them in his pocket with the others.

He should now tear out a few more matches and keep them hidden in his hand.

You now turn round, look at the number of matches remaining in the book, and tell him immediately how many matches he is holding in his hand.

How to do it: Simply subtract the number of matches left in the book from nine (e.g. if there are five matches left in the book, he has four in his hand; if there are two left, he has seven, etc.)

Make sure that there are only 20 matches in the book to start with though, otherwise the trick will not work.

2.2 Heads or tails?

Place some coins on a table (as many as you like). Turn your back and ask a friend to turn over one coin at a time, saying 'turn' whenever he does so. He can do it as often as he wants and turn over the same coin several times if he wants. He then covers one coin with his hand. When turning round, you will tell him if the covered coin is heads or tails.

How to do it: Before turning your back, count the number of heads showing. Add 1 to the number every time your friend says 'turn'. If the total is even (2, 4, 6, 8, etc.) the number of heads will be even (including the hidden coin).

If the total is odd (1, 3, 5, 7, etc.) the number of heads will be odd.

By looking at the other coins, you can easily tell if the covered one is heads or tails.

2.3 Finding the total

Turn your back and ask a friend to throw three dice on a table. Ask him to add the numbers on the top of the dice. Then ask him to pick up any one of the dice and add the total on the *bottom* of that die to the number he already has. Then, ask him to take the same die, to throw it, and to add the number it now shows to his total.

You can now turn round, pick up the dice, and announce the total sum.

How to do it: Before picking up the dice, add up the top numbers on all three dice and add 7 to that number.

e.g.

$$1 + 4 + 5 = 10$$
$$\underline{+\ 7}$$
$$17$$

Your friend's total must be 17.

2.4 Three heaps of matches

Turn your back and ask a friend to form three heaps of matches. The heaps must have the same number of matches (more than three). Ask your friend to give a number between 1 and 12. By giving orders to your friend, you must bring the number of matches in the middle heap to the number given by your friend. E.g. Your friend has chosen to make three heaps of seven matches.

He then calls the number 5. You must bring the middle heap to five matches.

How to do it: Ask your friend to take three matches from each of the two end heaps and to put them in the centre.

Then ask him to count how many matches remain in one of the end heaps and to take that number from the centre one.

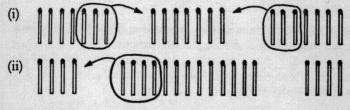

This always leaves nine matches in the middle heap. It is then easy to bring the total to the number given by your friend.

2.5 The three dice

Turn your back and ask a friend to put three dice on top of each other. Then ask him to add the numbers on faces of the dice that touch each other (see illustration) and that on the underside of the bottom die.

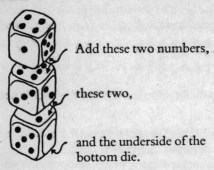

Add these two numbers,

these two,

and the underside of the bottom die.

You can then turn round and take out of your pocket a number of matches equal to the total found by your friend.

How to do it: Put 21 matches in your pocket first. Then take some out, leaving only a number equal to that showing on the face of the top die. E.g. (see illustration) the number showing on the die is 4. You leave four matches in your pocket and take 17 out, which is the total in this case.

2.6 Tell the numbers

Turn your back and ask a friend to throw three dice. Then ask him to do the following:
–take the number of one die and multiply it by 2
–add 5
–multiply the result by 5
–add the number of the second die
–multiply the result by 10
–add the number of the third die

Ask your friend what the total number is and you will be able to tell him what the three figures on the dice were.

How to do it: Subtract 250 from the total. The three figures of the number you get are those on the dice.

3 Magic

3.1

Can you hold a handkerchief by opposite corners and tie a knot in the centre without letting go of the ends you are holding?

How to do it: Fold your arms and take a corner of the handkerchief in each of your hands.

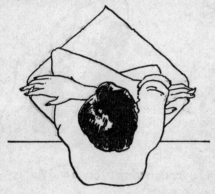

Then unfold your arms: a knot will immediately form.

3.2

Here is an unusual way of tying a knot. Try to do it in front of your friends and see if they can do it again. Although it is extremely easy to do, your friends will probably find it hard to imitate you.

Put the piece of string on a table and, holding end B with your right hand, put your left arm over end A and under end B.

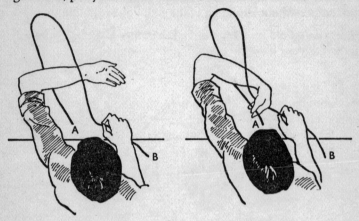

Then turn your hand over the string to catch end A.

When you draw your hands apart, a knot will form automatically.

3.3　The mysterious strips

Cut out three long strips of paper and join the ends of each strip to make three rings. They should be at least ½ cm wide and 1 or 2 m long. Take one of the strips and cut it along the centre:

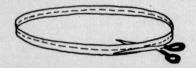

You will get two separate strips of the same length as the first one but half as wide:

Then ask a friend to do the same thing with another strip. To his astonishment, he will not get the same result, but will get two interlocked strips instead:

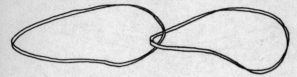

Ask him to try again with the third strip. This time, the result will be quite different: he will get one strip only, half as wide as the original one, but twice as long:

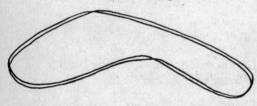

How to do it: Although the strips look the same, they are in fact slightly different. It is only their length which makes them appear similar.

Strip 1: an ordinary ring:

Strip 2: the two ends are joined after giving the strip half a twist:

Strip 3: give the strip a complete twist before joining the ends.

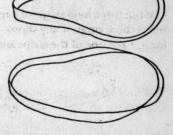

3.4 The walking hairpin

Put a hairpin over a ruler and let the pin touch a table top. If you incline the ruler a little so that the pin leans towards you, you will actually see it walk towards you. If the pin leans the other way, it will walk away from you!

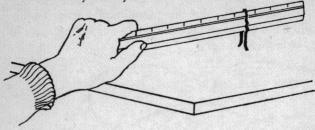

3.5 The hanging ring

Tie the two ends of a piece of string. Ask a friend to extend one of his hands and place the string over his middle finger and forefinger:

Without taking the string off your friend's fingers, can you put a ring on the string?

How to do it: Pull the string and put the ring on to it.

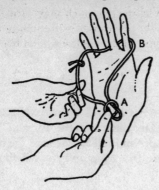

Pull on loop A and place it over your friend's thumb. Then remove loop B. The ring is now hanging from the string.

3.6 Upside down

Take a rectangular piece of paper with something written on it.
—Fold it lengthways

—Fold it again in half, folding the right half backwards

—Fold it again, this time folding the right half towards you

Unfold it and you will discover that your paper is upside down!

3.7   Black and white

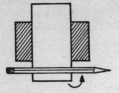

Cut two rectangular pieces of paper, one black and one white, about the size of a small bank note. Place them as in the diagram. Put a pencil on the white piece of paper and roll *both* around the pencil.

When you have finished, unroll the paper and you will find that the black one is now on top!

3.8   The middle of the ruler

Extend your two forefingers and balance a ruler on them.

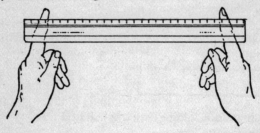

Slide your fingers beneath the ruler until they meet. You will find they *always* meet at the middle of the ruler, whatever you do.

Now try to do the opposite. Balance the centre of the ruler on your fingers and try to slide them back to the ends. You will find that one finger always remains at the middle of the ruler!

3.9 Freeing the scissors

Take a long piece of string (about 1 m) and tie its two ends. Then pass it through the two rings of a pair of scissors as shown on this diagram:

Ask somebody to hold the tied ends of the string.

Can you now take the scissors away without cutting or untying the string? If you do it under a scarf, it will seem even more mysterious.

How to do it: Pull in (a) so as to get a long loop and pass it through the right ring of the scissors, *under* the string already there. Then pass the scissors through this loop.

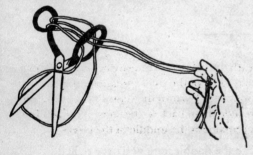

By pulling the two strings, you will free the scissors.

3.10 The moving ring

All you need for this trick is:
—a rectangular piece of wood or cardboard with a small hole in it
—a large ring or button (too big to go through the hole)
—a piece of string

Arrange them as follows, making sure that the string is well tied on each side of the piece of cardboard.

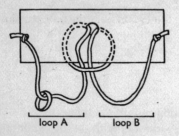

loop A   loop B

The problem is: without untying the string, can you move the ring from loop A to loop B?

How to do it:

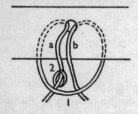

1. Loosen the middle loop by pulling it down
2. Push ring up
3. Hold ring and pull a and b towards you
4. Pass the ring through the double loop you have pulled
5. Pull the double loop back through the hole (by pulling from behind the piece of cardboard)
6. All you have to do now is to slide the ring down again. It is on loop B now.

3.11 The jumping rubber band

Put a long rubber band on your index finger:

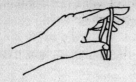

Then slip it around the middle finger and over the index again:

Ask a friend to hold the tip of your index finger and bend your middle finger as he does so. The rubber band will jump and hang from the middle finger only.

3.12 Linking paper clips

Here's one unusual method of linking two paperclips.

Take a strip of paper and, giving it the shape of an S, put two paperclips on it to keep it in that shape:

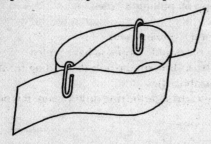

Pull the two ends of the paper. The clips will jump up and you will find them linked together.

3.13 One or two marbles?

Place two marbles on a table and show them to a friend. Then ask him to close his eyes and to cross the second and first fingers of one hand. Remove one of the marbles and put the tip of his two fingers on the remaining marble. Ask him how many he can feel. He will probably say 'two', and will be quite surprised when he discovers you have taken one away.

3.14 The wrong finger

Give a friend the following instructions:
–hold your arms in front of you
–cross them
–turn them so that your palms face each other
–clasp your hands tightly
–bend your elbows outwards
–bring your hands under your chin
Then point to one of his fingers (don't touch it!) and ask him to move it. You will probably find that he will move the wrong finger.

3.15 Cutting somebody in two

Wind a long piece of rope round a friend's waist. Then hold one end of the rope and ask somebody to come and hold the other end. At a signal, you must both pull the rope and you will see that it seems to cut through your friend.

How to do it: Stand behind your friend and, taking the rope over his head, hold it in front of him. He must then, as naturally as possible, put his hands behind his back, holding up one or two fingers. Although it seems that you are crossing the rope behind him, just loop each end over the fingers as you can see on this figure:

Then take the rope back in front of your friend and cross it.

3.16   The oracle

The following table can help you answer any question:

d	w	w	a	w	o	h	a	b	h
i	o	i	s	o	t	d	t	t	w
w	o	a	a	a	i	e	n	i	i
t	s	d	n	t	h	i	a	a	e
o	t	t	n	t	u	w	t	d	h
t	i	a	e	s	f	l	i	n	u
e	l	n	j	c	a	d	t	o	c
r	o	h	y	e	o	w	y	p	e
f	r	w	e	d	i	o	i	a	e
l	n	s	c	t	l	g	h	e	h

How to do it: Ask a friend for a question, e.g. 'Shall I be rich?'

Ask him to select a letter in the table. (Imagine he chooses the letter *b*, on the first line.)

Now, reading the table from left to right, select every fifth letter until you come again to the letter you started from. In this case you would get the following message: stainandenjoypeaceab.

You must now find where the message begins. Here, if you take out the last two letters and put them at the beginning, you can read the following answer to your question: 'Abstain and enjoy peace'.

3.17   The disappearing pen

Draw an empty hole with your hand in the air. You can draw it several times to make sure everybody can see it. Then take a pen and throw it through the hole. To everybody's surprise, the pen will disappear in the air!

How to do it: Just before throwing the pen, draw your hand back (as if it could give you more strength) and stick the pen at the back of your neck. It is better to practise the trick several times in order to get used to it.

3.18 Bending the pen

Take a pencil or a pen and show it to your friends. They can touch it to make sure that it's quite straight and not broken.

Then, by simply taking the pen and gently moving it, everybody will soon see the pen bending!

How to do it: Hold the pen between your thumb and forefinger $\frac{2}{3}$ of the way along:

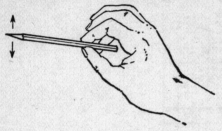

Then slowly start moving the pen up and down. This will give the impression that the pen is bending.

4 Playing with shapes

4.1

Draw the following shape on squared paper. Now cut along all the lines so that you have five pieces.

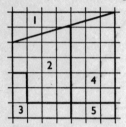

Now rearrange the pieces in this order:

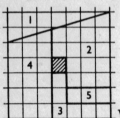

Where has the missing square gone?

Now cut out this shape:

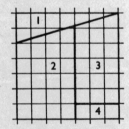

Can you rearrange these four pieces into a large square in such a way as to 'lose' one of the smaller squares?

4.2 The missing line

Draw a rectangle with 10 parallel lines in it. Then cut it along the diagonal as shown below:

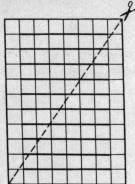

Slide one of the two parts along the line so as to get the following position:

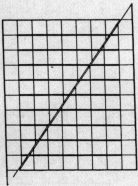

How many lines have you got now?
How can you explain it?

4.3 How to make a paper cat

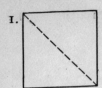 **1.** Start with a square. Fold the paper along the line, then unfold it.

 2. Do the same thing along the other diagonal.

3. Bend paper into this shape:

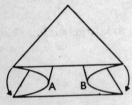

Press folds A and B.

4. Fold along AB and AC.

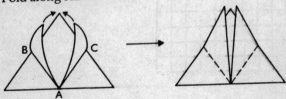

Then turn the paper over and do the same thing on the other side.

5. Fold along AB and AC.

Turn the paper over and do the same thing on the other side.

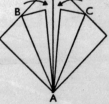

6. Unfold along AB and AC on both sides.

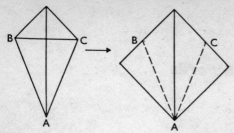

7. Fold DF to the centre (along DE). Press fold DE.

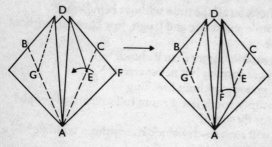

Do the same thing along DG and on the other side.

8. Unfold along DE and fold AF to the centre, along EA. Press fold EF and bring the point down towards D.

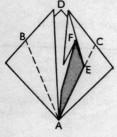

Do the same thing along AG and on the other side.

9. Cut off the bottom point below line AB.

Blow into the hole you have just made.

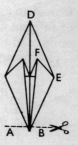

Part 2

5 Playing with words

5.1 Riddles

a) What has four legs and a back but cannot walk or move on its own?
b) What touches you all the time without being seen?
c) What can smile and move and laugh, just like you, without being alive?
d) What has a mouth bigger than its head?
e) What is always coming but never arrives?
f) What can't you say without breaking it?
g) Why is an empty room like a room full of married people?
h) Why do birds fly south?
i) How long will a seven-day clock run without winding?
j) What has four legs and flies?
k) What is the difference between a flea and an elephant?

5.2 Four errors

There is four errers in this centence. Can you find them?

5.3 A letter square

In this letter square, the word HER can be spelt in quite a number of different ways. You can start at any H and go left, right, down or up to an E, then to an R.

How many different ways can you find?

```
R E H E R
E R E R E
H E H E H
E R E R E
R E H E R
```

5.4 Tongue twisters

Can you say these tongue-twisters quickly?

—The cricket critic cricked★ his neck at a critical★ cricket match.
—There are thirty thousand feathers on that thrush's★ throat.
—I often sit and think
  And fish and sit
  And fish and think
  And sit and fish
  And think and wish
  That I could get a drink!
—Please, Paul, pause for applause.
—How many cookies could a good cook cook if a good cook could
  cook cookies?
—A canner★ exceedingly canny★
  One morning remarked to his granny,
  'A canner can can
  Anything that he can,
  But a canner can't can a can, can he?'

cricked: twisted, hurt
critical: important
thrush: a kind of bird
canner: someone who puts food in cans (tins)
canny: clever

5.5 What's the explanation?

a) A woman stopped in the street of the small town where she
    lived to light a cigarette. A man offered her a light, then invited
    her to his flat. As they entered the flat, he took off his coat. She
    suddenly exclaimed, 'You are the man who killed my
    husband!'

b) A man knocked on a door and opened it. Inside, another man
    was lying dead on the bed. On the floor was a small pile of
    sawdust★. The man who had come in was very pleased with
    what he saw.

c) While travelling across the desert I came upon a hut with a
    lorry parked outside. There was no furniture in the hut but

from a beam* high up in the roof a man was hanging by the neck.

d) While driving his son to work James Sanders had a terrible accident. He was killed on the spot. His son was badly injured and was rushed off to hospital. As he was being put on the operating table, the surgeon saw his face and cried out, 'But it's my son!'

e) During the revolution there was a curfew* and a total blackout during the hours of darkness to avoid aerial bomb attacks. Jason was a Negro. He wore dark glasses, black shoes and a black suit. The traffic in the main street was very heavy. None of the cars had their headlights on. Yet Jason walked out into the middle of the street and was unharmed. All the cars missed him quite easily.

f) It was two in the morning when I saw the car parked just off the motorway. A man was prowling* suspiciously round the car, looking on the ground. From inside the car I could hear screaming. Suddenly the man picked up a large stone and began to batter* the glass in the driving door.

> sawdust: the powder left after wood has been cut with a saw
> beam: a long piece of wood supporting the roof
> curfew: a time after which people must not go out
> prowling: walking like a wild animal
> batter: hit

6 Codes

6.1

The same message is hidden behind these five different secret codes:

a) DRONNAORTETIRTYBTROMGUONOVULTE
b) TUO OG OT YRT TON OD
c) ADON ROTT BRYT TOGO POUT
d) DTOONGOOTOTURTY
e) NODTTOTYROGOTUO

Can you find what the message is?
How would you write the following message in these five codes:
BEHIND THE HOUSE AT FIVE

6.2

You receive a message that says:
SEVEN TONIGHT IN GARDEN

This is what it looks like:
SNIIR ETGND VOHGE ENTAN

You want to write back:
YES TAKE KEYS AND WATER

How would you put it in the secret code?

6.3

Here is a secret code and a message:

A	B	C
D	E	F
G	H	I

J	K•	L
M	N	O
P	Q	R

S T V U (X pattern)   W• X Y Z (X pattern)

⌐⌐○> ⎕⌐○∨>⌐⚬⌐   ⊐⌐∨∟Ċ∧⚬⌐⚬<

a) Can you find out what the message is?
b) How would you transcribe: LEAVE YORK AT ONCE using the same code?
c) Can you work out the following message, based on a slightly different cipher/code:

⌐○○>)⌐ ∟○⌐∨⌐ ⎕⌐○>)⌐ ⎕<>⌐ >>⌐>

6.4

Here is a secret message. All you know is that one of the words is FIELDS. Can you find out what the complete message is?

PZZK KVZP MK KVZ XSJ QMBK XT KVZ ZMWK
WFJZ XL KZT MQBZ LFZSJW

The following message contains the word MONDAY:

TDDE TD LE EOD JMME MJ XMIK MHW EKDD
LE RFRD MR TMRWLX

What does it say?

Here is what is called a Vigenère table:

	D	I	S	C	O	V	E	R	Y	A	B	F	G	H	J	K	L	M	N	P	Q	T	U	W	X	Z
D	Z	X	W	U	T	Q	P	N	M	L	K	J	H	G	F	B	A	Y	R	E	V	O	C	S	I	D
I	X	W	U	T	Q	P	N	M	L	K	J	H	G	F	B	A	Y	R	E	V	O	C	S	I	D	Z
S	W	U	T	Q	P	N	M	L	K	J	H	G	F	B	A	Y	R	E	V	O	C	S	I	D	Z	X
C	U	T	Q	P	N	M	L	K	J	H	G	F	B	A	Y	R	E	V	O	C	S	I	D	Z	X	W
O	T	Q	P	N	M	L	K	J	H	G	F	B	A	Y	R	E	V	O	C	S	I	D	Z	X	W	U
V	Q	P	N	M	L	K	J	H	G	F	B	A	Y	R	E	V	O	C	S	I	D	Z	X	W	U	T
E	P	N	M	L	K	J	H	G	F	B	A	Y	R	E	V	O	C	S	I	D	Z	X	W	U	T	Q
R	N	M	L	K	J	H	G	F	B	A	Y	R	E	V	O	C	S	I	D	Z	X	W	U	T	Q	P
Y	M	L	K	J	H	G	F	B	A	Y	R	E	V	O	C	S	I	D	Z	X	W	U	T	Q	P	N
A	L	K	J	H	G	F	B	A	Y	R	E	V	O	C	S	I	D	Z	X	W	U	T	Q	P	N	M
B	K	J	H	G	F	B	A	Y	R	E	V	O	C	S	I	D	Z	X	W	U	T	Q	P	N	M	L
F	J	H	G	F	B	A	Y	R	E	V	O	C	S	I	D	Z	X	W	U	T	Q	P	N	M	L	K
G	H	G	F	B	A	Y	R	E	V	O	C	S	I	D	Z	X	W	U	T	Q	P	N	M	L	K	J
H	G	F	B	A	Y	R	E	V	O	C	S	I	D	Z	X	W	U	T	Q	P	N	M	L	K	J	H
J	F	B	A	Y	R	E	V	O	C	S	I	D	Z	X	W	U	T	Q	P	N	M	L	K	J	H	G
K	B	A	Y	R	E	V	O	C	S	I	D	Z	X	W	U	T	Q	P	N	M	L	K	J	H	G	F
L	A	Y	R	E	V	O	C	S	I	D	Z	X	W	U	T	Q	P	N	M	L	K	J	H	G	F	B
M	Y	R	E	V	O	C	S	I	D	Z	X	W	U	T	Q	P	N	M	L	K	J	H	G	F	B	A
N	R	E	V	O	C	S	I	D	Z	X	W	U	T	Q	P	N	M	L	K	J	H	G	F	B	A	Y
P	E	V	O	C	S	I	D	Z	X	W	U	T	Q	P	N	M	L	K	J	H	G	F	B	A	Y	R
Q	V	O	C	S	I	D	Z	X	W	U	T	Q	P	N	M	L	K	J	H	G	F	B	A	Y	R	E
T	O	C	S	I	D	Z	X	W	U	T	Q	P	N	M	L	K	J	H	G	F	B	A	Y	R	E	V
U	C	S	I	D	Z	X	W	U	T	Q	P	N	M	L	K	J	H	G	F	B	A	Y	R	E	V	O
W	S	I	D	Z	X	W	U	T	Q	P	N	M	L	K	J	H	G	F	B	A	Y	R	E	V	O	C
X	I	D	Z	X	W	U	T	Q	P	N	M	L	K	J	H	G	F	B	A	Y	R	E	V	O	C	S
Z	D	Z	X	W	U	T	Q	P	N	M	L	K	J	H	G	F	B	A	Y	R	E	V	O	C	S	I

As you can see, this one is based on the word DISCOVERY and the remaining letters of the alphabet, in order. If you decide on a code word, you can easily draw your own table. All you need, then, to code a message, is a second key-word (e.g. CATS)

    Message: LOOK IN MATTRESS
                CATS CA TSCATSCA

Then, you just read on your table the letters corresponding to:

L and C : E

O and A : G

O and T : D

K and S : Y etc.

Here, your coded message would read:

E G D Y T X H J I T W M Q J

a) Here's a message written with a similar code. What does it say?

    G A C V B Z D V L Y C V C Q Q

b) This is the answer to your message. This time, it uses the key-word HAPPY. What does it say?

K C V C O P Q V

c) Could you code the following message, using a table based on the word PRODUCTIVE and with the word JANE as a key-word?

STAY AT HOME DO NOT GET IN TOUCH WITH PETER

6.6

Here is a message: H P U W A X S C A A H J J S

What it means is: DO NOT TRUST DICK

Considering that in order to code it the number 41787 was used, can you find out what the method was?

Can you decode the following message, coming from the same person:

L F O I Z P J L L A S V Z ?

6.7

Can you find what numbers the letters stand for in these operations?

```
   B A B          B E S S E
 + K A K        -   G A G S
 ─────────      ─────────────
   C C C          B A S S
```

6.8

Look at this message:

R P Y M X Y I J N Y Q J A Q

Can you find out what it means, knowing that the following table was used:

```
B I R T H
D A Y C E
F G J K L
M N O P Q
S U V W X
```

6.9

AS UEH TFOLATI PACEH TS ITA HW?

a) SELEG NAS OL
b) KROYW EN
c) NO TGNI HSAW
d) OG ACIHC

6.10

a) Can you read the message concealed in this code?
   H E W B L T B M T L E S E B S F S O A F
   X E Z I A L Y E K H S R V A Q U B U G L

b) And this one?
   RENOA ONADM RTDEE DAGNY
   Can you work it out if you have the key?

S I M O N		I M N O S
T A K E C	S	A K C E T
A R E O N	I	R E N O A
M O N D A	M	O N A D M
Y D A N G	O	D A G N Y
E R T E D	N	R T D E E

7 Brainteasers

7.1

There are two cyclists 20 kilometres apart. They start to ride towards each other at the same moment. The road they are riding along is completely straight and they ride at 10 kilometres per hour. Just as they start, a fly on the forehead of one of the riders starts to fly towards the other rider at a speed of 15 kilometres per hour. It lands on the other rider's forehead and then turns round and flies back to the first rider. It keeps on doing this until it is squashed between the foreheads of the two riders when they meet. How far did the fly fly?

7.2

In a square room there was a cat in each corner, three cats in front of each cat and a cat on each cat's tail. How many cats were there altogether?

7.3

A woman pointed to the photograph of a man and said to her father, 'That man's mother was my mother's mother-in-law.' What was the relationship between the woman and the man in the photograph?

7.4

Harry has the habit of picking up cigarette ends left by other people. He knows that he can make one new cigarette out of seven ends. One Saturday night he collected 49 cigarette ends. The next day he made them into cigarettes and smoked them all.

How many whole cigarettes did he smoke that day?

7.5

A man took these five pieces of chain to a welder* to make into one long chain. The charge for cutting a link was 50p and for welding it to another link also 50p. The man paid £3 in all. How did he manage to pay so little?

welder: a man who joins pieces of metal

7.6

Joe hired a car to go to the horse races at Newmarket. It cost him £9. When he was half-way there he saw his friend Sid, so he picked him up and took him to the races. In the evening he dropped Sid off at the place he had picked him up. Then there was a terrific argument about how much Sid should pay Joe as his share of the cost of hiring the car. Joe said he should pay half but Sid, who had had less to drink, said . . .   What?

7.7

An expedition to explore the Lurgi desert is about to set off. It consists of four men and each one has enough food to last him five days. After some distance, one man gets sick and has to turn back. He takes with him just enough food to last him till he gets back to base. Then the second man does the same, and the third. How many days' journey was the last man able to make into the desert and get back safely? (You must assume that the men only travel in units of one day and that they can give food to the others.)

7.8

As I reached the ticket office I realised I had no cash, only a £10 postal order. The fare to Cambridge was £7 and the booking clerk would not accept my postal order. Luckily there was a pawnbroker* nearby, so I went in and pawned my postal order for £7. On my way back into the station, I met Patrick, a friend of mine, who offered to buy the pawn ticket from me for £7, to save me the trouble of coming back to London. Naturally I agreed, then rushed in and bought my ticket. When I got to Cambridge I still had £7 of course.

So who lost?

pawnbroker: someone who lends you money if you leave a valuable object with him

---

7.9

The ferry boat from Dingle to Dangle takes 5 minutes to cross when the tide is coming in and 15 minutes when the tide is going out.

How long does it take when no tide is running?

7.10

It takes a tourist spaceship 7 days to fly from Hexa to Gon. The Imperial Space Agency (I.S.A.) runs one ship per day which leaves at midday from Hexa. At the same time a return ship takes off from Gon. So whenever a ship is leaving Hexa or Gon, another one is just landing there, having arrived from the opposite direction. The ships follow the same space route. As I boarded my spacecraft at Hexa I wondered how many I.S.A. ships we would meet during our voyage. How many?

7.11

Amoebas are a very simple form of life and are able to reproduce very quickly. It only takes three minutes for an amoeba to reproduce itself. In the laboratory there were two jars of equal size. In one of them there were two amoebas. It took them 3 hours to fill the jar. As an experiment, I placed one amoeba in the second jar. How long did it take to fill the jar?

7.12

The famous chef Henri Labouffe had a problem. His staff had broken some of the kitchen crockery*. He had a jug full of vinegar but he only needed 4 decilitres. His only measuring jars were for 5 decilitres and 3 decilitres. So how did he manage to measure 4, without wasting any vinegar?

crockery: plates, cups, saucers, etc.

7.13

There were six glasses on the bar, three full and three empty.

The barman bet me £5 I could not make full and empty glasses alternate by moving just one glass. Would you have accepted the bet?

The gangsters have captured a rival. They intend to kill him but in order to make it more interesting, their leader says to him: 'Make any statement you like. If it's true, you'll be hanged. If it's false, you'll be shot.' What does the man say that saves him?

7.15

Two men played five games of chess. They each won the same number of games. How was this possible?

7.16

Three men with their wives come to a river. The boat they find can only take two people at a time. Because the men are all extremely jealous, no woman can be left with another man unless her own husband is also present. So how do they manage to cross the river?

7.17

Fred is Lord Stretching's gardener. Unfortunately his lordship is short of money and does not want to spend too much on his garden, though of course he wants it to look its best. Last year he bought 10 new cherry trees. He told Fred that he wanted them planted in five rows (lines) with four trees in each row. Fred scratched his head a while and then . . . what did he do?

7.18

Is it possible to cut this cake into eight equal pieces with just three cuts?

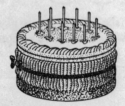

7.19

When farmer Jones died he left a herd of 17 cows. In his will he gave instructions that the cows were to be divided as follows: $\frac{1}{2}$ to his eldest son, Sam, $\frac{1}{3}$ to his second son, Michael, and $\frac{1}{9}$ to his youngest son, Benjamin. The three brothers could not see how this was possible. Luckily for them, a passing professor of mathematics heard of their problem and solved it for them. How?

7.20

Two Indians were talking to each other about family relationships. The fat one said to the thin one, 'Your father is my father's son.' 'That's right,' replied the thin one, 'and you yourself have neither sons nor brothers.' How were the two Indians related?

7.21

What is the weight of a standard pre-packed frozen pheasant if it weighs ¾ of a kilogramme plus ¾ of a standard pre-packed frozen pheasant?

7.22

Two men were standing facing in opposite directions. Yet each one could see the other without turning round. How was that possible?

7.23

Four suspects have been arrested on the charge of murdering Sylvia Forbes, the fashion model. Unfortunately they have been put in the wrong cells. Inspector Braine wants to interrogate each of them separately so that they have no chance to prepare an alibi between them. But he wants to start with A, then do B, C and D. How can the prisoners be moved so that A is in 1, B in 2, C in 3 and D in 4 without ever meeting each other and without wasting time? No prisoner may be left alone in the corridor of course, but the empty cell can be used.

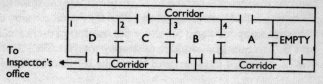

7.24

The security guard at the local bank spends the evening till midnight in the Manager's office. He then goes to bed in the store-room. In theory he should pass through all seven doors in the bank, locking each one behind him. In fact this cannot be done and he is always getting confused. The manager has therefore decided to build an eighth door so that he *can* pass through all the doors in succession, locking each one behind him. He is not quite sure where to put it however. Can you help? Remember the guard must start from the office and pass through every door *once* only before going to sleep in the store-room.

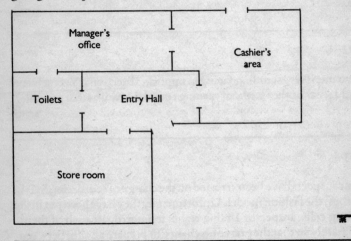

7.25

There were 500 soldiers lined up on the parade ground. They were in 10 rows of 50 columns. The sergeant-major called for the shortest man from each row to step forward. He chose the tallest of them and called him A. He then called for the tallest man in each column to step forward. He chose the shortest of them and called him B. The question is which of the two men is taller – A or B? (A was the tallest of the short and B was the shortest of the tall.)

7.26

Las Vegas is *the* place for gambling in America. I was just coming out of a Casino when a man came up to me and said 'I'll bet you $5 that if you give me $10, I'll give you $15.' What do you think I did?

7.27

Ali the thief had managed to break into the Sultan's treasure room. He was looking for a bag containing 1250 diamonds, each weighing 0.8 grams. Unfortunately, the Sultan had filled nine other bags with imitation diamonds. There were 1000 in each bag, each one weighing 1 gram. So all 10 bags weighed exactly 1000 grams and all the bags looked exactly alike. Just as Ali was scratching his head, the Sultan burst in with his guards. As he was a merciful Sultan, he gave Ali a chance to save his life. Here is what he said: 'If you can find the bag which contains the real diamonds by using these scales just *once*, you may keep the diamonds. If not, you will be beheaded. You can take stones from any of the bags and put them in other bags if you wish but you can only *weigh* once!'

How did Ali save his neck?

7.28

At the end of the canal there is a place for the barges to turn round. Unfortunately it is not very convenient since only the barges can pass under the bridge, whereas the lighters★ they are pulling cannot. The barge A needs to change the positions of lighter B and lighter C, so that B is where C is and C is where B is. Can this be done so that barge A finishes in its original position?

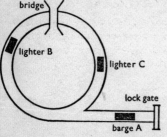

lighters: the boats which are pulled by barges

45

7.29

An employer was very anxious to find the most intelligent of the three men who had applied for a job. So he told them: 'Here are five conical hats. Three are white and two are black. I shall ask you to stand in 3 corners of the room facing the wall. I shall place a hat on each of your heads. When you turn round, you will be able to see the others' hats but not your own. The first one to tell me the colour of his own hat will get the job.' He then placed a white hat on each man's head. When the three men turned to face each other there was a long silence. Then, suddenly, one of the candidates said, 'Mine is white.' How did he know?

7.30

If the only sister of your mother's only brother has an only child, what is the relationship of that child to you?

7.31

Jack said, 'If I had one of your records, I'd have as many as you.' Bob said, 'If I had one of yours, I'd have twice as many as you!' How many records had each?

7.32

Yesterday my doctor prescribed* some tablets. There were five in the box. He told me to take one every half hour. How long did they last me?

prescribed: gave me

7.33

My two cousins Susie and Catherine were brought up to tell the truth at all times. But my aunt Jane, their mother, lets them tell one lie a year. Each can lie about the date of her birthday on her birthday only. On Christmas Day last year I asked them,

'When's your birthday?'

'Yesterday,' said Susie.

'Tomorrow,' said Catherine.

When I asked them the same question again on Boxing Day*, I got the same answers from them. So when are their birthdays really?

Boxing Day: the day after Christmas Day

7.34

The bus from Edinburgh to London left at 8 a.m. An hour later a cyclist started out from London for Edinburgh. When the bus and the cyclist meet, which of the two will be further from Edinburgh?

7.35

I wanted to fry some fish fingers for myself and my two guests. I had three fish fingers but the frying pan only holds two at a time. It takes 30 seconds to fry one side of a fish finger. So how did I manage to fry both sides of all three fish fingers in 1½ minutes?

7.36

How many times does the digit 9 appear between 1 and 100?

7.37

Can you arrange the numbers between 1 and 11 in the circles so that the total of the three numbers on each straight line is always the same?

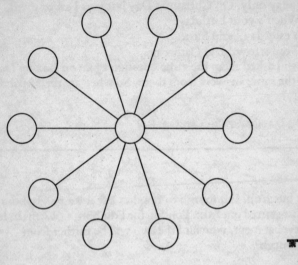

7.38

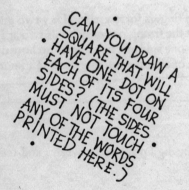

CAN YOU DRAW A SQUARE THAT WILL HAVE ONE DOT ON EACH OF ITS FOUR SIDES? (THE SIDES MUST NOT TOUCH ANY OF THE WORDS PRINTED HERE.)

The island of Grant is uninhabited except for the shepherd Bleat
and his flock of sheep. This summer, however, some campers
landed on the western end of the island. They were rather careless
and one day a fire broke out. The wind was blowing towards the
east and a wall of flames advanced quickly across the island
towards the eastern cape where Bleat was grazing his sheep. How
did Bleat save his sheep from burning or from jumping over the
cliff to their death?

8 Logical problems

8.1

There are three boxes labelled 'red balls', 'white balls' and 'red and white balls'. Each of the labels is incorrect. You are allowed to take one ball only from each box. How can you label each box correctly? (Of course, you are not allowed to look inside!)

8.2

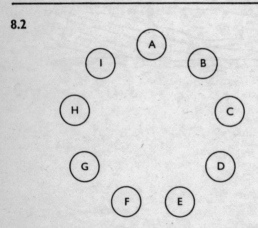

These nine men are surrounded by the enemy army. They are the last survivors of their army and have sworn★ to each other that they will die rather than surrender. To make quite sure that everyone dies, they agree to the following procedure: A, who is their leader, will shoot the person on his left, B. C will then shoot the person on his left, D. This will go on, with each survivor shooting the person on his left, till there is only one person left. He will then commit suicide. If you wanted to be the last person left alive, where in the circle would you have to stand?

sworn: promised

8.3

When Alex, Brian and Chris finished their race they were feeling very tired. It had been raining very heavily, so heavily in fact that the judges were unable to see who came in first, who second and who third. When he asked the three men, they each made two statements. One man lied in both his statements. The other two told the truth. This is what they said:

Alex said, 'I came in first. Chris was last.'
Brian said, 'Alex wasn't first. Chris came in second.'
Chris said, 'I was before Alex. Brian wasn't second.'
So what was the order in which they crossed the finishing line?

8.4

These three statements are true:
1. All camels have bad breath.
2. None of my friends is a camel.
3. Some of my friends smoke cigars.

Then which of the following statements (A, B, C)
i *must* be true?
ii *might* be true?
iii *cannot* possibly be true?

  A None of my friends has bad breath.
  B Camels who smoke cigars are friends of mine.
  C Some cigar smokers are not camels.

8.5

The local minibus that runs from our village to the nearest town has the following seating regulations:
Maximum capacity:
sitting: 8 adults or 12 children
standing: 2 adults or 4 children

As the last bus drew up at one of the stops on Saturday evening there were six adults who wanted to get on. But there were already seven children in the bus. How many of the adults would be able to get on the bus if the regulations were observed?

8.6

Here is a row of five shops in Blexdon:

The owners of these five businesses are:
Mrs Loan (who is not the house agent)
Mr Cherry (who is not the greengrocer)
Mr Fitting (who is not the tailor)
Mr Sweet (who is not the grocer)
Mr Glitter (who is not the jeweller)

Luckily we know that Mr Glitter owns one of the end shops in the row. We also know that Mr Fitting's shop is next to the grocer. Mr Fitting is also very friendly with the greengrocer and hopes that one day she will sell him her shop. So who is the owner of which shop?

8.7

Mr Jackson and his family (his son, his daughter and his sister) are very fond of playing bridge. They play at least twice a week and get very excited about who is the best player. Here is what we know about them:
–the best player's twin★ and the worst player are of opposite sexes
–the best player and the worst player are the same age
So who is the best player?

twin: brother or sister born on the same day

8.8

Johnson, Blake and Crispin work for British Airways. One is a pilot, one a navigator and one a cabin steward (but we do not know which one does which job).

In the aeroplane there are three passengers with the same surnames. We will call them Johnson 2, Blake 2 and Crispin 2. From the following information, is it possible to work out who is the pilot?
a) Crispin 2 lives in London.
b) The navigator lives in Birmingham.
c) Blake 2 wears spectacles.
d) The passenger whose name is the same as the navigator's lives in Brighton.
e) The navigator and one of the passengers who is a boxer, belong to the same football club.
f) Johnson beat the steward at cards.

8.9

I live in a very small village where many people are related to each other. For example Tom, Dick and Harry are garage owner, vicar and solicitor* but not in that order. Tom is the vicar's father-in-law and Dick is the solicitor's son-in-law. Everyone was at the church last Saturday when Harry married the garage owner's daughter. Who does which job? (By the way, the people are very moral in our village, so none of the three has been married more than once.)

solicitor: lawyer who prepares legal documents

8.10

When a machine was invented for going forwards or backwards in time, the inventor very wisely decided to consign* it to the world scientific authority. And the authority decided to organise an expedition into the future, sending the five best scientists available. Unfortunately, there was a language problem. Each of the scientists could speak two languages, but each language was only shared by two scientists.

One person speaks Dutch and Serbo-Croat but no one speaks both Norwegian and Chinese. B speaks Serbo-Croat and E does not speak Norwegian. One of the Japanese speakers can talk to D but not in Japanese.

B, D and E can speak all five languages between them. A and B have a language in common, but C and E do not.

Can you work out who speaks which languages?

consign: offer

8.11

When the Rajah's daughter was kidnapped, he arrested three young men. The suspects were brought before his wise old guru.

Ravi said: 'Gopal did it.'

Gopal said: 'But that's not true.'

Kushwant said: 'It was Ravi who did it.'

Ravi said: 'What Kushwant says next will be true.'

Gopal said: 'What Ravi has just said is false.'

Kushwant said: 'Ravi has made two false statements.'

The guru meditated for a few minutes before whispering the name of the guilty person in the Rajah's ear. Which name?

8.12

These four cards have been taken from two ordinary packs – one with red backs and one with blue backs. Two cards are face down and two face up:

Red back   Blue back

 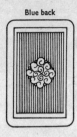  

The question is: 'Of these four cards, does every card with a red back have an ace on its other side?'

Which cards would you have to turn over to answer this question?

8.13

One evening there was a murder in the home of a married couple, their son and daughter. One of these four people murdered one of the others. One of the members of the family witnessed the crime.

The other one helped the murderer.

These are the things we know for sure:

1. The witness and the one who helped the murderer were not of the same sex.
2. The oldest person and the witness were not of the same sex.
3. The youngest person and the victim were not of the same sex.
4. The one who helped the murderer was older than the victim.
5. The father was the oldest member of the family.
6. The murderer was not the youngest member of the family.

Who was the murderer?

8.14

Here are eight empty circles in which you must put the numbers
1, 2, 3, 4, 5, 6, 7, 8.

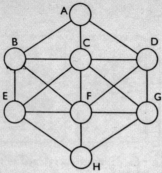

But you must not put two numbers following each other (e.g. 3
and 4, 6 and 7) in two circles that are adjacent or connected by a
line. In the following example, 3 and 4 should *not* be placed as they
are:

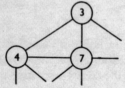

Can you do this?

8.15

At 10 o'clock one morning Mr Smith and his wife left their house in Connecticut to drive to the home of Mrs Smith's parents in Pennsylvania. They planned to stop once on the way to have lunch at a restaurant.

At 11 o'clock, Mrs Smith asked: 'How far have we gone, dear?'

Mr Smith looked at the meter: 'Half as far as the distance from here to the restaurant,' he said.

They arrived at the restaurant at twelve, had a good lunch and continued on their way. At 5 o'clock, when they were 200 kilometres from the place where Mrs Smith had asked her first question, she asked a second one: 'How much farther do we have to go, dear?' Mr Smith answered, 'Half as far as the distance from here to the restaurant.'

They arrived at their destination at 7 that evening. Because of traffic conditions Mr Smith had driven at very different speeds.

Can you tell exactly how far the Smiths travelled from one house to the other?

8.16

There are 13 cards on a table.
1. Each card is either a Queen, a Jack, a King or an Ace.
2. There is at least one Queen, one Jack, one King and one Ace.
3. The numbers of Jacks, Queens, Kings and Aces are all different.
4. There is a total of five Queens and Kings.
5. There is a total of six Queens and Jacks.

There were only two cards of one of the types of cards. Can you find which?

8.17

Eight dice have been left on a table in the relative positions shown on the diagram below:

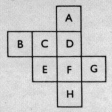

Of the numbers showing on the dice:
1. There is at least one 2.
2. Every 2 is between two 3s.
3. There is at least one 3 between two 5s.
4. No 5 borders on a 2.
5. There is exactly one 1.
6. No 3 borders on the 1.
7. At least one 3 borders on a 3.
8. Each die shows either a 1, a 2, a 3 or a 5.

Which one of the dice on the diagram shows 1?

8.18

Kingston has a grocery, a bakery and a bookshop. When I went to Kingston last week, the bookshop was open.
1. Those three shops are not open together on any day of the week.
2. The bakery is open 4 days a week.
3. The grocery is open 5 days a week.
4. All three places are closed on Sunday and Wednesday.
5. On three consecutive days:
   the bakery was closed on the first day
   the bookshop was closed on the second day
   the grocery was closed on the third day
6. On three consecutive days:
   the bookshop was closed on the first day
   the grocery was closed on the second day
   the bakery was closed on the third day

On which one of the days of last week did I go to Kingston?

8.19

The main street in Coffin Canyon was dusty and the sun shone down pitilessly as the seven bandits came out of the saloon. They had been drinking all morning and had got into an argument about who was the best shot. The only way to solve this problem was to go into the street and shoot it out. So they all staggered out into the blinding sun and took up position as in the diagram below Their names were Al, Butch, Chuck, Dude, Eric, Fred and Gus. You can see where they were standing from the diagram. As you can see, each man could take a shot at just two others. So without moving from their positions they began firing. Dude fell down dead first, shot through the head by Al. In fact Al was the only one left alive at the end of the battle. From this information you can work out who shot whom and in what order the six men were killed.

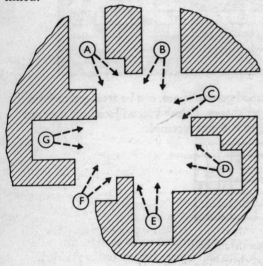

9 Manipulative problems

9.1 Pentominoes

There are 12 different ways you can arrange five squares edge to edge:

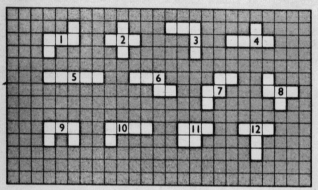

These 12 shapes, called pentominoes, can be arranged to form many different larger shapes. Below you will see how they are arranged to form a 10 × 6 unit rectangle:

Can you now arrange these pentominoes so as to form:
—a large square (with a smaller square left out in the middle):

—a large square with one square missing from each corner:

—a cross (only nine pentominoes are needed):

9.2 Piles of cans

Six cans have been piled on a board:

The problem is to move them, one at a time, from one board to another so as to arrange them in this way:

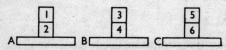

No can can rest at any time on another with a smaller number.

9.3 Getting in line

Rule a sheet of paper into squares and place three white buttons and a black one on it. The black one will remain in the position shown on the picture. The white ones can move.

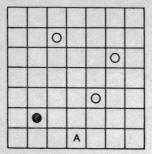

The problem is to arrange the white buttons so that each square will be in line (laterally or diagonally) with at least one button, black or white. It is almost the case in the picture as only the square marked A is not in line with one of the buttons.

9.4 Striking the dots

There are 25 dots in the figure below:

$$\begin{matrix} \bullet & \bullet & \bullet & \bullet & \bullet \\ \bullet & \bullet & \bullet & \bullet & \bullet \\ \bullet & \bullet & \bullet & \bullet & \bullet \\ \bullet & \bullet & \bullet & \bullet & \bullet \\ \bullet & \bullet & \bullet & \bullet & \bullet \end{matrix}$$

How many consecutive strokes are needed to strike all these dots? (Consecutive strokes are straight lines that must be drawn without removing the pen from the paper.)

9.5 Wrong flag

Here is the flag the king of Limaria had ordered:

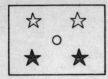

Unfortunately, this is the flag that was brought to him:

He tells the man who brings the flag that unless he sets it right by cutting out *one piece only* and putting it back, he will be beheaded.

What can the man do to save his head?

9.6 The sphinx

The following geometrical figure is called 'The sphinx'. Can you divide it into four equal parts, each one being in itself a small sphinx figure?

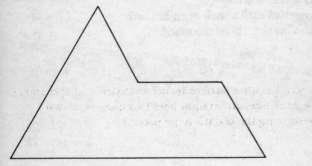

9.7 Four squares

If you place 16 matches as follows, you form five squares:

By moving three matches only, can you manage to get four squares of the same size?

Now consider the way these 16 matches are arranged:

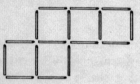

Can you move two of them so as to get four squares, three small and one large one?

9.8 Squares and triangles

You are given eight matches. Can you arrange them so as to get two squares and four triangles?
–The full length of each match must be used.
–You mustn't break or bend the matches.

9.9 Four square units

On the figure below you can see 12 matches forming a square. This square contains nine square units:

If you arrange these 12 matches in a different way, you can obtain a rectangle with an area of five square units only:

Can you now arrange the matches so as to form the perimeter of an area of four square units only? You must use the entire length of each match.

9.10 Tri-dominoes

A tri–domino is an equilateral triangle.

Using two of them, you can only obtain this shape:

Using three of them you can only form this shape:

How many different shapes can you obtain if you use four, and then five tri–dominoes?

9.11 The five matches

Here are the various distinct patterns you can obtain with one to four matches:

1: ⎯

2: ⎯ ⎯

3: △ ≤ Y

4: ▢ ≷ ╀ ᛏ Y

How many can you obtain with five matches?

Don't forget that:
—you cannot bend the matches
—they can only touch at their ends (don't cross one match over another)
—a pattern must be considered as elastic and can be deformed
  Therefore:

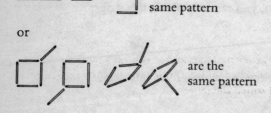

are the same pattern

or

are the same pattern

9.12 The six cigarettes

As you can see on the following diagram, it is very easy to arrange four balls so that each ball touches the other three:

But can you place six cigarettes so that each cigarette touches the other five? Make sure that you do not break or bend the cigarettes!

9.13 Heads and tails

Put 16 coins on a table, alternating heads and tails as shown below

● ○ ● ○

○ ● ○ ●

● ○ ● ○

○ ● ○ ●

By touching *two coins only* with your fingers can you re-arrange these coins so that you will have only heads or tails in each vertical column?

9.14 The cork

Can you lay down four matches and a cork on a table so that:
–the heads of the matches will not touch the table or the cork
–the cork will not touch the table

9.15 Reversing the order

Draw seven adjacent squares on a piece of paper and, leaving the one on the left empty, put six counters or papers number 1 to 6 on the other squares:

Can you reverse the order of these counters so as to get the following arrangement:

You can only:
—move into an adjacent empty square
—jump over the next counter into an empty square

Try to do if with the smallest number of moves!

9.16 From left to right

Take a rectangular piece of cardboard and cut out smaller pieces of cardboard that will fit on to it in the following way:

J	I	G
A	(hatched)	F
A	(hatched)	H
A	(hatched)	E
B	C	D

Can you move the pieces of cardboard so as to place A in the following position:

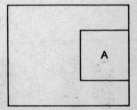

You are not allowed to take the pieces off the cardboard frame.

9.17 Tangram

Tangram is an old Chinese puzzle game.

In order to play it you need seven pieces of cardboard that can be rearranged into hundreds of shapes. First cut out a square piece of cardboard along these lines:

See how they can be made to form these shapes:

Can you now form the following ones:

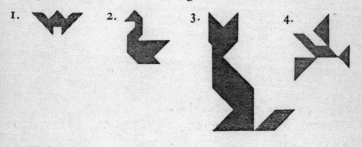

7.

8.

9.

10 Paradoxes

Paradoxes are fascinating because they state facts which, if they are true, must be false, and if they are false, must be true. Epimenides the Cretan made the statement: 'All Cretans are liars.' If it is true, then, because a Cretan made it, it must be false. And if it is false, then, because a Cretan made it, it must be true. Consider the following examples:

a) Please answer 'yes' or 'no' to the following question. Will the next word you speak be 'no'?

b) A: What B is just going to say is false.
   B: What A has just said is true.

c) A card had printed on one side of it: THE SENTENCE ON THE OTHER SIDE OF THIS CARD IS FALSE.
   On the other side was printed: THE SENTENCE ON THE OTHER SIDE OF THIS CARD IS FALSE.
   Imagine writing one of these sentences on each side of a strip of paper. If you made the paper into a Möbius strip, which would be the 'other' side?

d) 'There was only one catch and that was Catch-22, which specified that concern for one's own safety in the face of dangers that were real and immediate was the process of a rational mind. Orr was crazy and could be grounded. All he had to do was ask; and as soon as he did, he would no longer be crazy and would have to fly more missions. Orr would be crazy to fly more missions and sane if he didn't, but if he was sane he had to fly them. If he flew them he was crazy and didn't have to; but if he didn't want to he was sane and had to.'
   (Joseph Heller, *Catch-22*)

e) Chuang Tzu the ancient Chinese philosopher fell asleep. While asleep he dreamt he was a butterfly. When he awoke he did not know if he was a man who had dreamt he was a butterfly, or a butterfly who was now dreaming he was a man.

f) One friend said to another, 'Here are 10 boxes. Please close your eyes. While your eyes are closed I shall place a coin in one of them. Then I want you to open the boxes one at a time in order from 1 to 10. I guarantee you will find an unexpected coin in one of them. That is, you will not be able to work out in advance which box it will be in.'

The friend however was a logician. He reasoned like this: 'Obviously he will not put the coin in box 10, because if I have opened 9 boxes and found no coin, then the one I find in box 10 will be expected. But in the same way, he cannot put it in 9 either, since, if I open the first 8 boxes and do not find it, I shall know it is in 9 (as 10 has already been ruled out). The same reasoning in fact goes for all the boxes. So it is clearly impossible for me to find an unexpected coin.'

Yet when he found the coin in box 7, he was surprised just the same!

g) A problem arose when a man said to his wife: 'I'm going to surprise you on your birthday tomorrow. I'm going to give you an unexpected gift. It's the fur coat you saw in Harrod's last week.'

How is his wife to understand this? Her husband always keeps his promises. On the other hand, if he gives her the fur coat, it will not be a surprise. She does not know what to think. If he gives her the fur coat it will not be a surprise. If he does not give it to her, he will have broken his promise. Needless to say she's very surprised when on her birthday he gives her the fur coat.

Now try your hand at reasoning out these paradoxical problems.

10.1

A barber in a small village was once asked how good business was. 'Excellent!' he replied. 'Of course I don't shave people who shave themselves, but I shave all the others.'

Does the barber shave himself?

10.2

Protagoras was a Greek sophist who taught in the fifth century before Christ. He once told one of his pupils that the pupil could pay him only after he had won his first case. The young man studied and when he was at last ready for clients, he waited and waited, but nobody came. Protagoras was impatient for his money and told him he was going to drag him to court.

Here's Protagoras's argument:
–If I win the suit, I will get my money (because of the judgement of the court).
–If I lose the suit, my pupil will win, and so he will give me my money (because of the arrangement we made).

Here's his pupil's argument:
–If I win the suit, the court will let me go without paying you.
–If I lose, then I don't have to pay you: we said I would after winning my first case.

Who was right?

10.3

A waiter in a restaurant sees seven different customers come in. Each one insists on having a table for himself. Unfortunately, there are only six free tables left. Yet he promises he will arrange it for them. This is what he thinks: 'I'll take the first man to the first table and ask another one to join him for a time. Then I'll show the third man to the second table, the fourth man to the third table, the fifth man to the fourth table, the sixth man to the fifth table. Then I'll go back to the first table and take the seventh man to the sixth table.'

Do you think he really managed it?

10.4

Is there anything wrong with this young man's argument?

'Yesterday, I entered a bookshop and bought a £1 paperback which I paid for with a £1 note. When I came back home I realised I already had the book and went back to the shop the next day. I returned the first book and chose a book worth £2 instead.

'As I was going to leave the shop, the assistant called me and asked me for the £1 difference. But of course, I pointed out to him that I had given £1 on the preceding day and was returning the book which cost £1; so he had his £2.'

10.5

Two young men start a new job in an office. The manager tells them they will start with £4000 a year paid every half-year and have a choice of:

—a rise of £50 a year
—a rise of £20 every six months

One of the young men chooses the first option, the other the second one. How can you explain the fact that the manager gave the job that involved more responsibility to the young man who had chosen the second option?

10.6

Which would you rather have: a clock that has stopped, or a clock that gains 1 minute a day? You will obviously choose the clock that gives you more often the correct time.

Which one is that?

10.7

Three girls spent a night in a hotel and before leaving in the morning, they asked for the bill which amounted to £30. Each gave £10. A few minutes later, the manager realised he had made a mistake and should have asked for only £25. So, he sent the hotel boy to them with £5. The boy didn't see how he could possibly divide £5 between three people, so he kept £2 for himself and gave £1 to each of the girls. So each girl paid £10 − £1 = £9. Altogether they paid £9 × 3 = £27.

As for the hotel boy, he had £2. That's only £29.

Where did the missing pound go?

10.8

Fred: Today is not Monday.
Ted: That's true.
Jen: We have made one false statement between us.

What day is it then?

74

11   Probability problems

11.1

Alistair, Bryan and Charles have decided to fight a duel. They will use pistols and stand at the three corners of an equilateral triangle.

A

B   C

They will fire in turn in a given order until two men are dead. Among the three men:
A is a very good shot (he always hits what he aims at)
B is 75% successful
C is not such a good shot and is only 50% successful.

Who has the best chance of survival (independently of who shoots first)?

11.2

Your father has promised you a new tennis racquet if you win two games of tennis in a row. You will play on three afternoons against your father and your mother alternately. You can choose whom you are going to play against first. You know that your father plays better than your mother. In what order would you decide to play the games?

Father		Mother
Mother	or	Father
Father		Mother

11.3

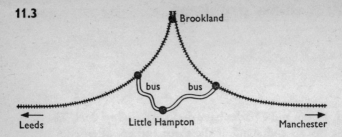

Brookland

bus   bus

← Leeds   Little Hampton   Manchester →

A man lives in Brookland and works in the village of Little Hampton. In order to go to work he either takes the Leeds or the Manchester train, gets off at the next stop and takes a bus to Little Hampton. He always takes the first train that comes (there are the same number of trains in both directions – one every 10 minutes – and the bus is always ready to leave when he arrives at the next stop).

He goes to work at very different hours every day. How can you explain that, 9 times out of 10, he finds himself on a Manchester train?

11.4

It was 4 o'clock in the morning and I had to catch a train at 5. As I did not want to wake my wife by putting on the bedroom light I took my clothes into the bathroom to dress. Then I realised I had forgotten my socks. I only wear black or green socks and I knew that, as I am very untidy, there were 10 green socks and 20 black socks all mixed up in the drawer. So I went back into the dark bedroom and took some socks out of the drawer. What is the smallest number I would have to take to be sure of having a pair of matching colour?

11.5

You have just wrapped four gifts for your friends in different—coloured papers and you are about to write your friends' names on them before putting them under the Christmas tree. Unfortunately, the lights suddenly go out. The gifts are all the same size and you can't recognise them in the dark. However you decide to write names at random on them, hoping they might be right by mere chance.

What is the probability that each of your friends will get the present you bought for him?

11.6

In his story called *The Lady or The Tiger?* Frank Stockton describes a cruel king who had a strange way of administering justice. The prisoner was put in an area in which there were two doors. Behind one was a hungry tiger, behind the other was a young lady. The prisoner had to open one of the doors. So he was either devoured by the tiger or, if he opened the other door, he married the girl.

One day, the king discovered his daughter loved a young man: he immediately arrested him and had him brought into the arena. The king's daughter was there. She knew that behind one door was a tiger and behind the other was a lovely lady who loved the young man. Of course, the king's daughter hated her. She knew behind which doors the tiger and the lady were.

When the young man was brought into the arena she made a sign with her right hand. The young man went to the door on the right. Who was behind: the lady or the tiger?

11.7

Here is a prediction that will work in many cases. It has been discovered that if you ask somebody to choose a number between 1 and 5, they have a tendency to choose the number 3. If you ask for a number between 1 and 10, they will very often select the number 7. So you can try the following experiment:

Write the number 37 on a piece of paper and ask a friend to select a two–digit number between 0 and 50. The two digits must be different (not 11 for instance) and both must be odd.

You will find that 37 is likely to be selected!

Clues 🗝

Codes

6.1 Try these two possibilities:
    –reading the code backwards
    –reading only one letter out of two, or three . . .
    This should help you find what the message is. It will then
    be easier to find out what the five different codes are.

6.2 Try arranging the message in a rectangle
    (20 letters = five four-letter lines).

6.3 Study the position of the letters in relation with the lines,
    e.g. ⅂ = G.

6.4 Find which of the words in the code has the same number of
    letters as FIELDS. Then try substituting the letters in that
    word and wherever the same letters appear in the message.
    You will see you can already guess what some of the words
    mean . . .

6.8 Try breaking up the letters in groups of two and look at their
    place in the table.

6.9 Try reading backwards.

6.10 Don't read all the letters in each line.
    Don't read one line *after* the other.

Brainteasers

7.1 The two riders met after one hour. How far can the fly fly in
    an hour?

7.2 How many corners are there to a room?

7.3 Who was her mother married to?

7.4 Do not forget that the cigarettes he has made will also produce cigarette ends.

7.5 What will happen if he opens the three links on one piece only?

7.7 Call the men A, B, C and D. Suppose that A feels ill at the end of the first day. He goes back next day. He therefore uses up two days' food and has three left. He gives each of his friends one day's food each. So on the second day, B, C and D still have five days' food each. Suppose that at the end of the second day B feels ill. He needs two days' food to get back but gives his two companions one day's food each . . . now go on.

7.8 If the man who travelled to Cambridge had been able to use his £10, he would have had £3 left after deducting the fare. Instead he has £7. So £4 has come from somewhere. In order to redeem* the postal order, someone will have to pay the pawnbroker back his £7 . . .

7.10 First try to work out how many space-ships there are in the whole fleet. Logically we must meet all the ships, except our own.

7.11 After 3 minutes, there are two amoebas in the second jar too.

7.12 Start by filling the 5 decilitre container. Then fill the 3 decilitre container. This leaves 2 decilitres in the 5 decilitre container. Then pour the 3 decilitres back into the jug . . .

7.13 What about pouring?

7.14 He must find something which is true if it is false, and false if it is true.

redeem: get back

7.15 Who were they playing?

7.16 Start off by A taking his wife across and coming back alone.

7.17 Think of a star with five points.

7.18 The cuts do not have to be in the same plane*.

7.19 Suppose there had been 18 cows, how many each would the sons have got?

7.21 So $\frac{1}{4}$ of the pheasant weighs $\frac{3}{4}$ of a kilo.

7.22 Which way were they looking if they could see each other?

7.23 Start by moving A into the empty room, and C into room 4.

7.24 It will be in one of the walls of the manager's office. Which one?

7.26 What would be the result if he lost the bet?

7.27 Suppose there were only three bags. If Ali took one stone from bag no. 1, two from bag no. 2, and three from bag no. 3, and weighed them together, would he be able to tell which was the bag of diamonds?

7.28 A's first move will be to put lighter C in the straight piece of canal near the lock gate. Lighter B can then be pulled or pushed into C's former position. But then what?

7.29 There are three possible combinations: two men had black hats and one a white one (this must be excluded because if one man had seen two black hats, he would *immediately* have known his was white); two had white hats and one had a black one; all three had white hats.
  The secret is to work out the colour of one's own hat from what the *other* people must be able to see.

in the same plane: in the same direction

7.30 Look for the answer in a mirror.

7.31 Try out one or two possible answers. For example, suppose Jack has three records, and Bob five. Then if Bob gives him one, each will have four. But if Jack gives one to Bob, he has six and Jack has only two. So that will not work. Try another pair of numbers in the same way.

7.32 Shorter than you think.

7.33 Remember that only one of the answers given by each girl can be true.

7.34 When two things meet they are in the same place.

7.35 Obviously I could not do it by frying two on one side and then on the other. Suppose I had fried two on one side and then taken one out and replaced it with the third?

7.36 More often than you think.

7.37 Put six in the middle circle. Then try to make the three figures in each line add up to 18.

7.38 Think of one box inside another box.

7.39 Sometimes it is necessary to go towards a danger.

Logical problems

8.1 It will be sufficient to correctly identify one box. We *know* that all the boxes are incorrectly labelled. Once one box has been correctly identified, all we need to do is to switch the labels on the other two boxes.

8.2 Make a diagram for yourself and eliminate the people as described.

8.3 What Alex and Brian say about Chris disagrees. Therefore one of them must be lying.

8.4 Think carefully about what is included in a definition, what is excluded by it and what is not covered by it.

8.5 If 12 children can sit in the same space as eight adults, how much room would three children take up?

8.6 Since we know that Mr Glitter is not the jeweller and yet owns one of the end shops, he is clearly the house agent. Mrs Loan should also be easy to place, as she is the only woman . . .

8.7 First work out how many people are the same age. When you know this you will know who the twins are – Mr Jackson and his sister, or his children. One of the twins is the best player . . .

8.8 There are two related sets of information: one about where people live, one about what they do. Try to separate these first. One way of doing this is to construct matrices:

	Pilot	Navigator	Steward
Johnson			×
Blake			
Crispin			

	London	Birmingham	Brighton
Johnson 2	×		
Blake 2	·×		
Crispin 2	√	×	×

We can gradually complete these using the information given.
e.g. We know Johnson cannot be the steward (from (f)).
We also know Crispin 2 lives in London.

8.9 Work out first of all who the various people cannot be. For example, Dick cannot be the solicitor because he is his son-in-law.

8.10 Make a matrix and try to work out who speaks what:
e.g. B speaks Serbo-Croat

82

D does not speak Japanese
E does not speak Norwegian

	Japanese	Dutch	Serbo-Croat	Norwegian	Chinese
A					
B			√		
C					
D	x				
E				x	

8.11 The key sentences are Ravi's 'What Kushwant says next will be true' and Kushwant's 'Ravi has made two false statements.' Work back from there.

8.12 Read the question very carefully. Is there an ace on the back of every red-backed card? Does every card without an ace have a red back?

8.13 Establish what we know about the youngest person first. This person cannot have been either the victim three, the helper four or the killer five. Then work out who was oldest, youngest, etc. After this draw up the various possibilities about who could have been what.

8.15 Forget about the times, they are irrelevant. When the first question is asked they are $\frac{1}{3}$ of the way between the start and the restaurant ($\frac{2}{3}$ left to go). When the second question is asked they are $\frac{2}{3}$ of the way between the restaurant and the finish.

8.16 First of all work out all the possible combinations of numbers to satisfy conditions 1, 2 and 3. Which of these can be eliminated by conditions 4 or 5 – or the last sentence of the problem?

8.17 Work out the different possibilities for placing two. One of these will fit all the conditions.

8.18 Draw up a grid with the shops and the days marked on it:

	Sunday	Monday	Tuesday	Wednesday	Thursday	Friday	Saturday
Grocer	Closed	Open	Open	Closed	Open	Open	Open
Baker	Closed			Closed			
Bookshop	Closed			Closed			

Fill it in with the information given, and use the conditions to work out the rest.

8.19 First of all work out who must have been the *last* person to die. Then work backwards.

Solutions

4.1

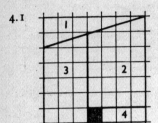

5.1
a) A chair
b) The air
c) Your picture in a mirror
d) A river
e) Tomorrow
f) The word 'silence'
g) Because there isn't a single person
h) Because walking would take too long
i) It won't run
j) A dead horse
k) An elephant can have fleas, but a flea can't have elephants

5.2
a) There **are**
b) errors
c) sentence
d) The fourth error is the fact that there are only 3 errors in the sentence

5.5 These are all satisfactory answers to the problems. There are others however – and yours may be just as good.
a) Her husband had recently been hanged for murder. The man was the local hangman. When he took off his coat, he hung it in a cupboard. She saw his hangman's mask hanging in the cupboard.
b) Both men were dwarfs in a circus. The one on the bed was smaller than the other one and therefore enjoyed more prestige in the circus. He also had a wooden leg. The bigger dwarf was jealous of him, so to get his revenge he waited till the smaller one went to sleep, leaving his wooden leg next to the bed. He then sawed off a part of the leg. When the smaller dwarf woke up, he screwed his leg back on and tried to walk. In his confusion

he thought that he had grown. This gave him a heart attack and he fell back dead on the bed.

c) The man had transported a big block of ice to the hut. He climbed on it, tied the rope round his neck and the beam and waited till the ice block melted.

d) The surgeon was a woman – his mother.

e) It was day time.

f) The man had locked himself out of his own car by accident. Inside his young son was screaming because he had his fingers caught in the safety belt.

6.1 DO NOT TRY TO GO OUT

a) BAETHRIONEDITSHEETHEORUISTEVABTUFSIEVNEE

b) EVIF TA ESUOH EHT DNIHEB

c) ABEH RIND ATHE THOU ISEA ATFI OVER

d) BOEUHSIENADTTFHIEVHE

e) BEH   IND   THE   HOU   SEA   TFI   VEZ

HEB   DNI   EHT   UOH   AES   IFT   ZEV

HEBDNIEHTUOHAESIFTZEV

6.2   YEST
AKEK
EYSA   YAENT EKYDE SESWR TKAAZ
NDWA
TERZ

6.3   a) INTERESTING DISCOVERY

b)

c)

A	B	C
D	E	F
G	H	I

WILL COME AT ONCE BRING STONES

6.4   MEET THEM AT THE OLD CART ON THE EAST SIDE OF TEN ACRES FIELDS

MEET ME AT THE FOOT OF YOUR OLD TREE AT NINE ON MONDAY

6.5 a) BRING MONEY IN PUB
   b) WHICH PUB?
   c)

	P	R	O	D	U	C	T	I	V	E	A	B	F	G	H	J	K	L	M	N	Q	S	W	X	Y	Z
P	Z	Y	X	U	S	Q	N	M	L	K	J	H	G	F	B	A	E	V	I	T	C	U	D	O	R	P
R	Y	X	W	S	Q	N	M	L	K	J	H	G	F	B	A	E	V	I	T	C	U	D	O	R	P	Z
O	X	W	S	Q	N	M	L	K	J	H	G	F	B	A	E	V	I	T	C	U	D	O	R	P	Z	Y
D	W	S	Q	N	H	L	K	J	H	G	F	B	A	E	V	I	T	C	U	D	O	R	P	Z	Y	X
U	S	Q	N	M	L	K	J	H	G	F	B	A	E	V	I	T	C	U	D	O	R	P	Z	Y	X	W
C	Q	N	M	L	K	J	H	G	F	B	A	E	V	I	T	C	U	D	O	R	P	Z	Y	X	W	S
T	N	M	L	K	J	H	G	F	B	A	E	V	I	T	C	U	D	O	R	P	Z	Y	X	W	S	Q
I	M	L	K	J	H	G	F	B	A	E	V	I	T	C	U	D	O	R	P	Z	Y	X	W	S	Q	N
V	L	K	J	H	G	F	B	A	E	V	I	T	C	U	D	O	R	P	Z	Y	X	W	S	Q	N	M
E	K	J	H	G	F	B	A	E	V	I	T	C	U	D	O	R	P	Z	Y	X	W	S	Q	N	M	L
A	J	H	G	F	B	A	E	V	I	T	C	U	D	O	R	P	Z	Y	X	W	S	Q	N	M	L	K
B	H	G	F	B	A	E	V	I	T	C	U	D	O	R	P	Z	Y	X	W	S	Q	N	M	L	K	J
F	G	F	B	A	E	V	I	T	C	U	D	O	R	P	Z	Y	X	W	S	Q	N	M	L	K	J	H
G	F	B	A	E	V	I	T	C	U	D	O	R	P	Z	Y	X	W	S	Q	N	M	L	K	J	H	G
H	B	A	E	V	I	T	C	U	D	O	R	P	Z	Y	X	W	S	Q	N	M	L	K	J	H	G	F
J	A	E	V	I	T	C	U	D	O	R	P	Z	Y	X	W	S	Q	N	M	L	K	J	H	G	F	B
K	E	V	I	T	C	U	D	O	R	P	Z	Y	X	W	S	Q	N	M	L	K	J	H	G	F	B	A
L	V	I	T	C	U	D	O	R	P	Z	Y	X	W	S	Q	N	M	L	K	J	H	G	F	B	A	E
M	I	T	C	U	D	O	R	P	Z	Y	X	W	S	Q	N	M	L	K	J	H	G	F	B	A	E	V
N	T	C	U	D	O	R	P	Z	Y	X	W	S	Q	N	M	L	K	J	H	G	F	B	A	E	V	I
Q	C	U	D	O	R	P	Z	Y	X	W	S	Q	N	M	L	K	J	H	G	F	B	A	E	V	I	T
S	U	D	O	R	P	Z	Y	X	W	S	Q	N	M	L	K	J	H	G	F	B	A	E	V	I	T	C
W	D	O	R	P	Z	Y	X	W	S	Q	N	M	L	K	J	H	G	F	B	A	E	V	I	T	C	U
X	O	R	P	Z	Y	X	W	S	Q	N	M	L	K	J	H	G	F	B	A	E	V	I	T	C	U	D
Y	R	P	Z	Y	X	W	S	Q	N	M	L	K	J	H	G	F	B	A	E	V	I	T	C	U	D	O
Z	P	Z	Y	X	W	S	Q	N	M	L	K	J	H	G	F	B	A	E	V	I	T	C	U	D	O	R

JANE IS NEWS HE HAS SEEN ME JANE ANEW ANEW

JEWMPEMHMTDHLGPDREZXUGOBWNZAWJXARH

6.6   D O   N O T   T R U S T   D I C K
      4 1   7 8 7   4 1 7 8 7   4 1 7 8
      H P   U W A   X S C A A   H J J S

HE HAS LIED TO US

6.7 $232 + 434 = 666$
     $10550 - 9295 = 1255$

6.8   Break the message into groups of two letters:
     RP YM XY IJ NY QJ AQ
     Imagine that they form two corners of a rectangle in the table.
     The two letters they correspond to are the other two corners of that
        rectangle.
     RP → TO
     YM → DO   etc.
     → TO DOVER   GO ALONE

6.9 What is the capital of the U.S.A.?
    a) Los Angeles
    b) New York
    c) Washington
    d) Chicago

6.10 HE WILL BE THERE AS USUAL
TAKE CARE ON MONDAY   DANGER   TED

7.1 It flew 15 kilometres.

7.2 There were four cats.

7.3 The woman was either the man's daughter or his niece.

7.4 He made eight cigarettes.

7.5 By cutting open the three links of one piece only and joining the other four pieces.

7.6 Here is one possible solution:
Distance covered by Joe:

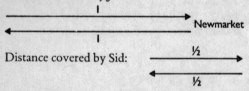

Distance covered by Sid:

Sid has therefore travelled $\frac{1}{3}$ of the complete distance travelled by Joe (1 out of 3 units) and should pay $\frac{1}{3}$ of the price, that is to say £3. Can you think of any other answers to this problem?

7.7 He was able to take four days to go and four to come back.

7.8 Patrick is the loser.

7.9 It takes $7\frac{1}{2}$ minutes.

7.10 We would see 15 spaceships. The space fleet is made up of 16 ships. Of course we do not meet our own.

7.11 It takes 3 hours and 3 minutes for the second jar to be filled.

7.12 Then pour the 2 decilitres into the 3 decilitre container. Refill the 5 decilitre container. Pour 1 decilitre into the 3 decilitre container, thus filling it. 4 decilitres are left in the 5 decilitre container.

7.13 Pick up glass no. 2 and pour it into glass no. 5. Replace the now empty glass no. 2.

7.14 He says 'I will be shot.' If this is true then he will be hanged, but he cannot be hanged because he cannot then be shot, and it would not then be true, and he could not therefore be hanged . . .

7.15 They were each playing someone different (not each other).

7.16 A takes his wife across and returns alone. Then B's and C's wives cross together. A's wife comes back. B and C then cross over and B comes back with his wife, leaving C and his wife on the far side. A and B then cross and C's wife returns. A's and B's wives now cross. C rows back and fetches his wife.

7.17

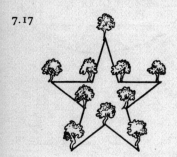

7.18

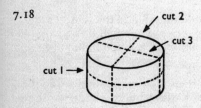

7.19 The professor of mathematics suggested they add one imaginary cow before doing their division:

$\frac{1}{2}$ of 18 = 9
$\frac{1}{3}$ of 18 = 6
$\frac{1}{9}$ of 18 = 2
————
17

Curiously enough, as you can see, this adds up to 17!

7.20 The thin one was the daughter of the fat father.

7.21 It weighs 3 kilos.

7.22 They were facing each other.

7.23 The changeover could be done in 10 moves.
A to Empty, C to 4, D to 2, B to 1, A to 3, C to Empty, D to 4, B to 2, A to 1, C to 3.

7.24 The new door would have to be at 6.

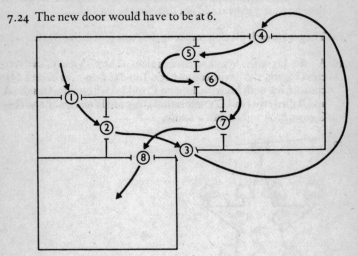

7.25 B will always be taller than A. That is, the shortest of the tall will always be taller than the tallest of the short.

7.26 I told him to go and look for another fool to try it on! If I had accepted his bet and given him the $10, he would simply have said 'I lose the bet.' He would then have given me the $5 he had bet me. But I would have lost the other $5 through my stupidity.

7.27 Ali put the bags in a row and removed one stone from the first bag, two from the second, three from the third, etc. He therefore had 55 stones. If all the stones weighed 1 gram, the total weight would be 55 grams. But Ali knew that some were 0.2 grams lighter. So supposing the total weight had been 54.6 grams, he would have known that it was bag no. 2 which contained the diamonds (53 stones at 1 gram and two stones at 0.8 gram each = 1.6 grams). If the total had weighed 54.2 grams, he would have known it was the fourth bag he was looking for (51 stones at 1 gram and four stones at 0.8 gram each = 3.2 grams). In this way he could locate the bag with the real diamonds with no trouble at all.

7.28 A picks up C and pushes it into the lock. A then goes round under the bridge and pushes B into the lock too. The two lighters are then linked together and A pulls them out on to the left-hand portion. The lighters are then separated again and A pushes B into the lock. It then pulls C into the left-hand portion. A returns under the bridge to pull B out of the lock and to push it into the right-hand portion. A then returns to the lock.

7.29 He could see two white hats. Therefore he might have had on either a white or a black hat. He then reasoned like this: Suppose my hat is black. If it is, my two rivals A and B can each see a black hat and a white hat. One of them (A) might then work out that his own hat could not be black because, if it were, B would see two black hats and would know that his own hat must therefore be white. B says nothing however. A might therefore conclude, if my hat is black, then his own hat must be white. But since he does not come to this conclusion, then my assumption that my hat is black must be false. Therefore my hat must be white.

7.30 The child is yourself.

7.31 Jack has five records and Bob has seven.

7.32 They lasted two hours.

7.33 Susie's birthday is on Christmas Day.
Catherine's is on Boxing Day.
On Christmas Day Susie answered 'yesterday'. On Boxing Day she also answered 'yesterday'. If her first answer had been true, then her second would also have had to be true (because it was given on a day not her birthday). This is therefore impossible, and her first answer was false; her second, true. Her birthday is therefore on Christmas Day.
Similarly for Catherine.

7.34 The bus and the cyclist are exactly the same distance from Edinburgh of course.

7.35 I put in two and fried them on one side (30 seconds). I took one out, turned one over and put the third in (30 seconds). Now I had one cooked on both sides and two cooked on one side. So I turned over the one in the pan and put back the one I had taken out earlier (30 seconds) and all three were cooked.

7.36 It appears 20 times.

7.37

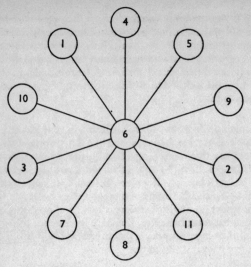

7.38

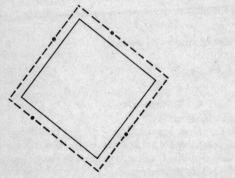

7.39 He drove them *towards* the fire. He then lit a fire on the cape. This quickly burnt the grass so that he was able to drive the sheep back on to it. So by the time the big fire arrived there was nothing left to burn.

8.1 The first thing to do is to take a ball from the box incorrectly labelled 'red and white balls'. If it is red, then clearly this is the box containing red balls. If white, then white. Since we know that the boxes are all incorrectly labelled it is now sufficient to switch the two remaining labels.

8.2 You would have to stand at C.

8.3 Alex and Brian say different things about Chris. Therefore one of them is lying and Chris must be telling the truth. Since Chris says he was before Alex, it is obvious that Alex is lying about coming first. Therefore the real order must have been Brian (who wasn't second, according to Chris who told the truth), then Chris (because Brian said so, and he also was telling the truth) – finally Alex.

8.4 A. *might* be true, since bad breath is not restricted to camels and none of the statements excludes the possibility of my friend's sharing this disagreeable characteristic.
   B. *cannot* be true, since none of my friends is a camel.
   C. *must* be true because some of my friends smoke cigars and none of them (see 2) are camels.

8.5 No problem! If 12 children can sit in the same space as eight adults then three children could sit in the space for two adults. This meant that if four children stood up and three remained seated, there would still be room for the six adults to sit down. So everyone was able to get on.

8.6 *Mr Glitter* who is not the jeweller owns an end shop. So he must be the *house agent*.
   Mrs Loan must be the *greengrocer* because we know Mr Fitting hopes to buy *her* shop (she is the only woman).
   Mr Fitting, who is not the tailor, is next to the grocer. Since he is not the tailor, he must be the *jeweller*.
   Mr Sweet, since he is not the grocer, must be the *tailor*.
   And *Mr Cherry* is therefore the *grocer*.

8.7 We know that twins are the same age, and that the best and the worst player are the same age. Therefore three players are the same age. So the daughter, the son and the sister are all the same age, since Mr Jackson must be older than his children. His children must be the twins referred to therefore. One of them is the best player. Since the best and worst players are the same age, the worst player must be Mr Jackson's sister. And since the worst player and the best player's twin are of different sexes, the best player must be Mr Jackson's daughter.

8.8 This is a problem which can be solved by constructing matrices:

	Pilot	Navigator	Steward			London	Birmingham	Brighton
Johnson			×		Johnson 2	×		
Blake					Blake 2	×		
Crispin					Crispin 2	✓	×	×

Starting from (f), we know that Johnson cannot be the steward. We therefore put a cross in the top right hand box on the left matrix.

We also know that Crispin 2 lives in London, so we put a tick in the bottom left hand corner of the right matrix, and crosses in the same column and line – to show that neither Johnson nor Blake lives there.

We know from (b) that the navigator and the boxer live in the same town (they support the same club). We also know from (c) and (e) that the boxer cannot be Blake 2 (because he wears spectacles). So he must be Johnson 2. We can now complete the right hand matrix. Johnson 2 lives in Birmingham, so Blake 2 must live in Brighton. Now to the left matrix. We know from (d) that the navigator must be Blake (he has the same name as the passenger who lives in Brighton). We therefore place a tick in the central box of the matrix and crosses in the same line and columns. This leaves only one box empty for the steward – Crispin, and after that for the pilot, Johnson.

	Pilot	Navigator	Steward			London	Birmingham	Brighton
Johnson	✓	×	×		Johnson 2	×	✓	×
Blake	×	✓	×		Blake 2	×	×	✓
Crispin	×	×	✓		Crispin 2	✓	×	×

8.9 We know that Tom cannot be the vicar (because he is the vicar's father-in-law), that Dick cannot be the solicitor (he is his son-in-law) and that Harry cannot be the garage owner. We also know that Tom is not the garage owner, Dick is not the vicar and Harry is not the solicitor ('not in that order'). So Tom must be the solicitor, Dick the garage owner and Harry the vicar. The vicar is of course already married, but it is one of his jobs to marry other people!

8.10	Japanese	Dutch	Serbo-Croat	Norwegian	Chinese
A	√	✗	✗	√	✗
B	✗	✗	√	√	✗
C	✗	√	√	✗	✗
D	✗	√	✗	✗	√
E	√	✗	✗	✗	√

8.11 The second statement which Ravi makes is impossible because it states that what Kushwant will say next will be true. Clearly if Kushwant says 'Ravi has made two false statements' and one of them was that what he himself has just said is false, then something is wrong. So Ravi's second statement is false (and so is Kushwant's). But if Ravi's first statement is also false, then Kushwant's second statement would be true. So clearly Ravi's first statement is true. Gopal did it.

8.12 You have to turn over the red–backed card and the Queen of Hearts. In order to answer the question you must find out whether there is an ace on the other side of the red card, and whether the Queen of Hearts has a red back. If either of these is the case, the answer to the question is 'No'. If it is not, the answer is 'Yes'.

8.13 We know from (3) that the youngest person was not the victim, from (4) that the youngest person was not the helper and from (6) that the youngest person was not the killer. The youngest person can only have been the witness therefore. If we make up a chart there are now three possible combinations:

```
Oldest person (father)      H    H    M
Next to oldest (mother)     V    M    H
Next to youngest (son)      M    V    V
Youngest (daughter)         W    W    W
(H = helper; V = victim; M = murderer; W = witness)
```

We can work out from (5) that the father was the oldest, from (2) that the youngest person must have been the daughter. Therefore the next to youngest must have been the son and the next to oldest, the mother.

Of the three possibilities: the first is impossible (from (3) – the youngest person and the victim were of different sexes); the third is also impossible (from (1) – the witness and the helper were of different sexes). Therefore only the second possibility holds – and the *mother* was the murderess.

8.14

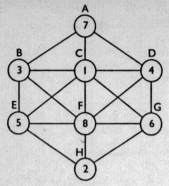

8.15 The answer is 300 kilometres.

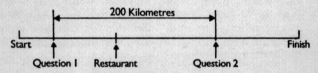

The times are irrelevant. From question 1 we can work out that the distance from question 1 to the restaurant is ⅔ of the total distance from the start to the restaurant. From question 2, we can work out that the distance from the restaurant to the point where the second question was asked is ⅔ of the distance from the restaurant to the finish. Clearly therefore the distance between the questions (200 kilometres) is ⅔ of the total distance – 300 kilometres.

8.16 Using the information from (1), (2) and (3) the only possible combinations of cards are:
i)   1, 2, 3, 7
ii) 1, 2, 4, 6
iii) 1, 3, 4, 5

We can eliminate (iii) because there is no 2 in it (we know there are only two cards of one type). We can also eliminate (i) because no two numbers add up to six (we need a total of six Queens and Jacks). Therefore (ii) must be the correct combination: one King, two Jacks, four Queens, six Aces.

8.17 Starting with conditions (1) and (2) there are four possible positions for the 2. It could only be at C, F, C and F, or D.
If it is at C:

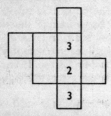

Then we cannot satisfy condition (7).
If it is at F:

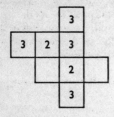

Then condition (3) cannot be satisfied.
If it is at C and F:

```
        ┌───┐
        │ 3 │
    ┌───┼───┼───┐
    │ 3 │ 2 │ 3 │
    └───┼───┼───┘
        │   │ 2 │
        └───┼───┤
            │ 3 │
            └───┘
```

Conditions (3) or (4) cannot be satisfied.
The only combination which will fit is if 2 is at D:

```
        ┌───┐
        │ 3 │
    ┌───┼───┼───┐
    │ 5 │ 1 │ 2 │
    └───┼───┼───┼───┐
        │ 5 │ 3 │ 5 │
        └───┼───┼───┘
            │ 3 │
            └───┘
```

8.18

	Sunday	Monday	Tuesday	Wednesday	Thursday	Friday	Saturday
Grocer	Closed	Open	Open	Closed	Open	Open	Open
Baker	Closed	Closed	Open	Closed	Open	Open	Open
Bookshop	Closed	Open	Closed	Closed	Closed	Closed	Closed

When completing the grid we first of all fill in closed for all shops on Sundays and Wednesdays. The grocer must also be open for the five remaining days (3). The baker must also be closed on Mondays to comply with (5) and (6). (Bakery closed Monday, bookshop Tuesday, and grocer Wednesday: bookshop closed Saturday, grocer Sunday and baker Monday.) We know from (2) that the baker must remain open on Tuesday, Thursday, Friday and Saturday. But since all three shops cannot be open on one day, the bookshop must be closed on Thursday and Friday too. In fact it only opens on Mondays – and that was the day I went to Kingston.

8.19 The last person to die was E since A had already shot D and the only other person he could see was E who obviously did not kill A since A is the only one left alive. Once this is established you can work backwards through the problem. E can only have shot B (because he couldn't shoot A); B could only have shot F, because B was still alive to shoot him, etc.
So the order is:
C shoots G
F shoots C
B shoots F
E shoots B
A shoots E

9.1

9.2 You need 60 moves to solve this problem!

1–b, 2–c, 1–c, 3–b, 1–a, 2–b, 1–b, 4–c, 1–c, 2–a, 1–a, 3–c, 1–b, 2–c,
1–c, 5–b, 1–a, 2–b, 1–b, 3–a, 1–c, 2–a, 1–a, 4–b, 1–b, 2–c, 1–c, 3–b,
1–a, 2–b, 1–b, 6–c, 1–c, 2–a, 1–a, 3–c, 1–b, 2–c, 1–c, 4–a, 1–a, 2–b,
1–b, 3–a, 1–c, 2–a, 1–a, 5–c, 1–c, 2–b, 1–b, 3–c, 1–a, 2–c, 1–c, 4–b,
1–b, 2–a, 1–a, 3–b.

9.3

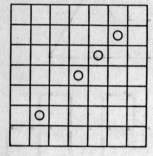

9.4 You need to make eight strokes.

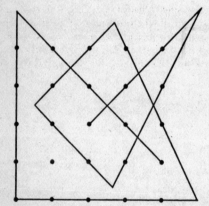

9.5 The dotted piece should be cut out, turned over, and sewn back:

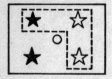

99

9.6

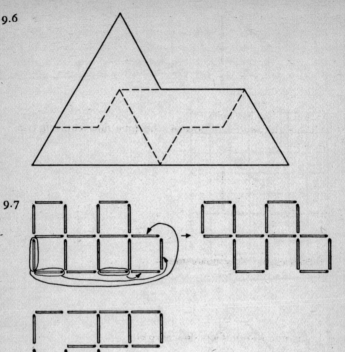

9.7

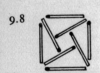

9.8

9.9

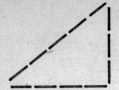

= area of 6 square units.

Change the position of three matches (nine thus removing two squares):

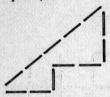

this area is now of 4 square units.

9.10 Using four tri-dominoes: four shapes:

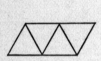

Using five tri-dominoes: five shapes:

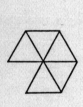  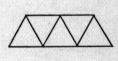

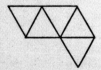

9.11

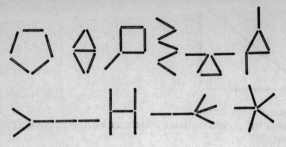

9.12

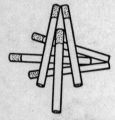

9.13

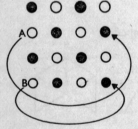

Put two fingers on coins A and B and bring them round to the other side, pushing the other coins to the left.

9.14

cork

9.15 You need to make 21 moves – in this order:
2 4 6 5 3 1 2 4 6 5 3 1 2 4 6 5 3 1 2 4 6

9.16

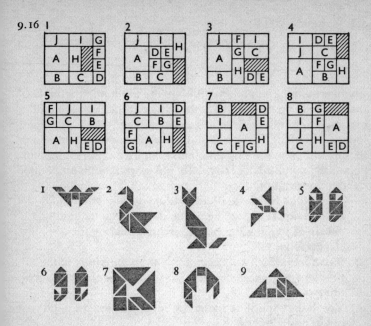

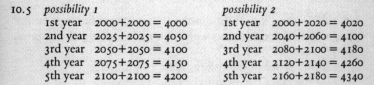

10.5

	possibility 1	
1st year	2000+2000 =	4000
2nd year	2025+2025 =	4050
3rd year	2050+2050 =	4100
4th year	2075+2075 =	4150
5th year	2100+2100 =	4200

	possibility 2	
1st year	2000+2020 =	4020
2nd year	2040+2060 =	4100
3rd year	2080+2100 =	4180
4th year	2120+2140 =	4260
5th year	2160+2180 =	4340

10.6 It will take the clock that gains 1 minute a day the number of minutes in 12 hours – that is to say 720 minutes – to be right again. As it gains 1 minute a day, it will be right only once every 720 days! But the clock that doesn't work will at least be right twice a day.

To the teacher

If you are a teacher, you may wish to use this book to stimulate discussion in your class. It has the advantage of provoking the expression of real opinions and points of view. The texts are no longer something to be read, understood and commented on, but the key to the resolution of problems in which the learners become personally involved. The pay-off in pedagogical terms can come in the development of:

i) The speech functions needed for group discussion and decision-making, e.g. agreeing, disagreeing/suggesting a course of action/proposing alternatives/asking for clarification.

ii) Structures which arise necessarily from the nature of the problem, e.g. conditionals/time-tense sequences/positional phrases.

iii) Vocabulary specific to certain types of problems, e.g. playing cards, numbers, dates.

Most of the activities in this book are best done either in pairs or in groups. For classroom use, we have found those in part 2 to be the most successful.

Here is one possible way of exploiting a problem:

–Divide the class into groups of four students.

–Distribute the problem to each group. Each group is given five minutes to formulate questions to ask the teacher. The questions should be ones to clarify the nature of the task, vocabulary problems, etc.

–Give a further 10 minutes in which the groups discuss among themselves possible solutions. Each must arrive at an agreed solution by the end of the 10 minutes.

–When time is up, each group in turn gives its solution to the whole class. There are always differences of opinion at this stage and groups must be prepared to defend their solutions.

(An alternative way of doing this is to send one member of each group to the next group and ask him to explain his group's solution to the new group.)

It is also possible to use part 1. One way of doing this would be to distribute a different activity to each group. After a set period of time, one member from each group has to go to another group to demonstrate the activity.

Language functions

It is possible to make generalisations about the kind of language functions which will be needed in order to arrive at a conclusion, then defend it. The suggestions below refer to the activities in part 2.

a) TRANSACTIONAL LANGUAGE (language used to organise the way the discussion takes place)
   –Getting started
      e.g. Right.
           O.K.
           Now then, . . .
           Let's see . . .
   –Making suggestions/proposals for a course of action
      e.g. Let's . . .
           Perhaps we could try . . .
           Why don't we . . .
           We could . . ., I suppose.
           If we . . ., the . . .
   –Giving directives
      e.g. You do the counting.
           Stop talking!
           Will you . . .
           Perhaps you could . . .
   –Negotiating agreement
      e.g. O.K.?
           All right?
           Is that all right then?
           Everyone agree?
           Any problems?
   –Summarising
      e.g. So, first of all . . .
           Now, . . .
           So, what we've got is . . .
           Let's go over it again.

b) DISCUSSION LANGUAGE (language used to talk about the
subject under discussion)
  —Stating opinion (about which one is more or less certain)
    e.g. It's obvious. It's . . .
         I think/I believe/suppose . . .
         It must/might/could/can't be . . .
         Perhaps/maybe, it is . . .
  —Agreement
    e.g. That's right.
         Of course, yes.
         I think so too.
  —Disagreement
    e.g. No.
         I don't think so.
         Are you sure?
         But if you . . .
         It can't . . ., because . . .
  —Asking for information
    e.g. What is . . .
         How many/much/old . . .
         Is it X or Y?
  —Asking for an opinion
    e.g. What do you think?
         Do you think that's all right?
         All right?
  —Asking for confirmation
    e.g. It's . . ., isn't it?
         And it was . . ., yes?
  —Asking for clarification
    e.g. How?
         What?
         What time?/How many?

c) REPORTING AND JUSTIFYING (when groups are explaining
their solutions)
  —Cause/effect
    e.g. When . . ., then . . .
         As soon as . . .
         Because . . ., then . . .
  —Logical deduction
    e.g. If . . ., then . . .

Because . . ., then . . .
Therefore . . ./so . . .
Must be/can't be
That's why . . .
- –Stating alternatives
e.g. It's either . . . or . . .
If it isn't . . ., then it is . . .
It can only be X or Y.
- –Time sequence
e.g. First . . .
Then . . .
Next . . .
Finally . . .
After that . . .
In the end . . .
Before/after
As soon as . . .

Since we know that much of this language will be required in group problem-solving activities, the question arises how – if at all – should it be introduced?

It might be tempting to conduct full-scale lessons to teach students, for example, all the ways of agreeing and disagreeing, how to defend your point of view, etc. It would also be extremely tedious and, as experience has shown, unproductive. What has proved more successful, at least in our experience of using these techniques, is to introduce some of the key language very briefly, just before the activity (e.g. on memo cards). While the activity is going on, the students are at liberty to refer to the cards. Little by little, they will learn to do without them. When the activity is over we have found it better not to analyse and correct the language performance immediately, but unobtrusively to return to points of difficulty in subsequent weeks.